INTRODUCTORY LEVEL Six-Way Paragraphs
in the Content Areas

INTRODUCTORY LEVEL Six-Way Paragraphs
in the Content Areas

100 Passages for Developing
the Six Essential Categories of Comprehension in the
Humanities, Social Studies, Science, and Mathematics

based on
the work of
W a l t e r
P a u k

JAMESTOWN PUBLISHERS

a division of NTC/CONTEMPORARY PUBLISHING GROUP
Lincolnwood, Illinois USA

Readability
Passages 1–25: Level D
Passages 26–50: Level E
Passages 51–75: Level F
Passages 76–100: Level G

ISBN: 0-8092-0371-5

Published by Jamestown Publishers,
a division of NTC/Contemporary Publishing Group, Inc.
4255 West Touhy Avenue, Lincolnwood (Chicago), Illinois 60712-1975 U.S.A.
© 2001 NTC/Contemporary Publishing Group, Inc.

2 3 4 5 6 7 8 9 10 11 12 113 09 08 07 06 05 04 03 02 01

Contents

To the Student

To succeed in the courses you take, one of the most important skills you can have is good reading ability. Depending on the content, different courses require different types of reading. For example, if material is easy for you or if you have studied it before, you may read it quickly. If the material is new or difficult, you may need to read more slowly. In fact, you may need to read it several times. In all the courses you take, you will be able to use the reading skills featured in this book.

The passages in the book are readings in four general categories: the humanities, social studies, science, and mathematics. Each category has several subcategories. For example, social studies may include passages in areas such as history, geography, and anthropology. Mathematics may include consumer and computer topics and puzzles as well as basic mathematical facts. Humanities passages deal with literature, music, art, and architecture.

Certain subject areas may be unfamiliar to you. But this book does not require you to master many new facts. Instead, its purpose is to show you *how to read in the content areas.* You will learn techniques that textbook writers use to organize material. You will see how new information can be applied to things you already know. And you will learn about the six skills that can help you read just about anything.

The Six Types of Questions

In this book, the basic skills necessary for reading factual material are taught through the use of the following six types of questions: main idea, subject matter, supporting details, conclusion, clarifying devices, and vocabulary in context.

Main Idea. While reading anything it is a good idea to ask yourself, What point is the writer trying to make? Once you ask this question, your mind will be looking for an answer, and chances are that you will find one. But if you don't focus in this way, all things seem equal. Nothing stands out.

Try to find the main idea in the following science passage by asking, What point is the writer trying to make?

There are four main kinds of salmon. One is the chinook. A big one can weigh 100 or more pounds. A fish like this could snap your rod. Second, there's the sockeye. It weighs about five pounds. Its flesh is deep red. This is the most important commercial salmon. It yields the highest dollar value. Pink salmon are the smallest. They weigh about three to seven pounds. Most pinks have a delicate flavor and are primarily caught for canning. Fourth is the coho. Its flesh is medium red. Coho usually weigh about nine pounds, but if they stay out at sea longer they can weigh up to 25 pounds.

A good answer here is, There are four main kinds of salmon. This passage is fairly easy to figure out because the first sentence is an excellent topic sentence.

The next example, from social studies, does not have a topic sentence. Nevertheless, the question What point is the writer trying to make? can still be answered. This time, think about the passage and come up with your own answer.

Most people traveled the Oregon Trail by covered wagon. Inside the wagon were all their possessions. Women and children usually rode and slept in there. Wagons had canvas tops. These were soaked in oil, which made them rainproof. Usually oxen pulled the wagons. People brought these animals along to plow their new farms. But the oxen couldn't climb well. They had to be pushed up mountain passes. Often wagons got stuck in the mud. Then people would have to lighten the wagons. Sometimes this meant throwing out possessions. If there was no bridge across a river, the oxen had to drag the wagons through the water.

This passage may have required a bit more thought, for the correct answer is a summary type answer. Compare your answer with the following main idea statement: Travel along the Oregon Trail was often difficult.

Subject Matter. This question looks easy and often is easy. But don't let that fool you into thinking it isn't important. The subject matter question can help you with the most important skill of all in reading and learning: concentration. With it, you comprehend and learn. Without it, you fail.

Here is the secret for gaining concentration: After reading the first few lines of something, ask yourself, What is the subject matter of this passage? Instantly, you will be thinking about the passage. You will be concentrating. If you don't ask this question, your eyes will move across the lines of print, yet your mind may be thinking of other things.

By asking this question as you read each passage in this book, you will master the skill so well that it will carry over to everything you read.

Let's see how this method works. Here is a short passage from science:

> The moon circles Earth on the average of once every 29 days. Its orbit around Earth is not circular; it is more of an oval. So the moon's distance from Earth can vary quite a bit. Sometimes it is about 250,000 miles from Earth. Other times it is only 220,000 miles away.

On finishing the first sentence your thought should have been something like, *Ah, a passage on the moon going around Earth. Maybe I can learn something about this process.* If it was, your head was in the right place. By focusing right away on the subject matter, you will be concentrating, you will be looking for something, your attitude will be superb, and, best of all, you will be understanding, learning, and remembering.

Supporting Details. In common usage, the word *detail* has taken on the meaning of "something relatively unimportant." But details are important. Details are the plaster, board, and brick of a building, while main ideas are the large, strong, steel or wooden beams. A solid, well-written passage must contain both.

The bulk of a factual passage is made up of details that support the main idea. The main idea is often buried among the details. You have to dig to distinguish between them. Here are some characteristics that can help you see the difference between supporting details and main ideas.

First, supporting details come in various forms, such as examples, explanations, descriptions, definitions, comparisons, contrasts, exceptions, analogies, similes, and metaphors.

Second, these various kinds of details are used to support the main idea. The words themselves—supporting details—spell out their job. So when you have trouble finding the main idea, take a passage apart sentence by sentence, asking, Does this sentence support something, or is this the thing being supported? In other words, you must not only separate the two but must also see how they help one another. The main idea can often be expressed in a single sentence. But a sentence cannot tell a complete story. The writer must use additional sentences to give a full picture.

The following social studies passage shows how important details are for providing a full picture of what the writer had in mind.

> The Amazon is the mightiest river for this reason. It discharges the greatest amount of water. More water flows out to sea than from the Nile, Mississippi, and Yangtze rivers combined. That's a lot of fresh

water! The force of its current is great too. The current can be seen 200 miles out in the sea. Here's a story to show the Amazon's amazing current. A sailing ship was far out of sight of Brazil. It ran out of drinking water. A passing ship drew alongside. The captain of the first ship asked for water. The captain of the second ship said, "Just dip your buckets over the side."

Here the main idea is in the first two sentences. Having stated the main idea, the writer goes on to give example after example showing why it is true. These examples are supporting details.

Conclusion. As a reader moves through a passage, grasping the main idea and supporting details, it is natural for him or her to begin to guess an ending or conclusion. Some passages contain conclusions; others do not. It all depends on the writer's purpose. For example, some passages simply describe a process—how something is done. It is not always necessary to draw a conclusion from such a passage.

In some passages with conclusions, the writer states the conclusion. But in most passages in this book, the conclusion is merely implied. That is, the writer seems to have come to a conclusion but has not stated it. It is up to you to draw that conclusion.

In the following science passage, the writer strongly implies a conclusion but does not state it directly.

The groundhog is a native American. It is found in most states east of the Rockies. It may also appear as far north as Alaska. It is hated by farmers. The groundhog eats a third of its weight in a day. What an enormous appetite! It may eat about a half-ton of alfalfa in a summer. So 10 chucks in a big field would eat five tons.

From this passage, we can draw the conclusion that the reason farmers hate groundhogs is that they destroy crops.

Sometimes a writer will ask you to draw a conclusion by applying what you have learned to a new situation, as in the following passage.

Odd as it sounds, orange growers use ice to fight freezing! Some spray their crops with water on a freezing night. The water freezes quickly, and then a strange thing happens. As long as ice stays wet, it can't get colder than 32 degrees Fahrenheit. Trees and oranges can stand this temperature. If the ice ever became entirely frozen and dry, it might drop many degrees and ruin the crop. The trick is to continually spray water on the ice. The spraying keeps the temperature from going below 32 degrees even if the air is much colder. This strange kind of "ice blanket" works only on plants strong enough to stand the weight of frozen spray.

If you were given a choice of what kind of growing thing this procedure would not work on, you would have to use your outside knowledge to pick the correct answer, delicate rose bushes.

Looking for a conclusion puts you in the shoes of a detective. While reading, you have to think, Where is the writer leading me? What conclusion will I be able to draw? And, like a detective, you must try to guess the conclusion, changing the guess as you get more and more information.

Clarifying Devices. Clarifying devices are words, phrases, and techniques that a writer uses to make main ideas, subideas, and supporting details clear and interesting. By knowing some of these clarifying and controlling devices, you will be better able to recognize them in the passages you read. By recognizing them, you will be able to read with greater comprehension and speed.

Transitional or Signal Words. The largest single group of clarifying devices, and the most widely used, are transitional or signal words. For example, here are some signal words that you see all the time: *first, second, next, last,* and *finally.* A writer uses such words to keep ideas, steps in a process, or lists in order. Other transitional words include *however, in brief, in conclusion, above all, therefore, since, because,* and *consequently.*

When you see transitional words, consider what they mean. A transitional word like *or* tells you that another option, or choice, is coming. Words like *but* and *however* signal that a contrast, or change in point of view, will follow.

Organizational Patterns. Organizational patterns are also clarifying devices. One such pattern is the chronological pattern, in which events unfold in the order of time: one thing happens first, then another, and another, and so on. A time pattern orders events. The event may take place in five minutes or over a period of hundreds of years.

There are other organizational patterns as well. Writers may use spatial descriptions to tell what things look like. They may use lists of examples to make their point. In science writing, they may use scientific data. Seeing the organizational pattern will help you read the material more easily.

Textual Devices. Textbook writers in particular use patterns or particular text styles to make their ideas clear. Bulleted lists, subheads, and boldfaced or italicized words help to highlight important ideas in the text. Charts or diagrams help you to visualize concepts more easily than if they are just explained in words.

Literal Versus Figurative Language. Sometimes a writer's words do not mean exactly what they seem to on first reading. For example, a writer may say, "The great tragedy shattered the hero of the story." You may know *shattered* as meaning "breaking into pieces." The word is often applied to breakable objects, but here it is applied to a person's feelings. Being alert to such special meanings of words can help you better appreciate the writer's meaning.

Two literary devices that writers use to present ideas in interesting ways are similes (SIM-a-lees) and metaphors (MET-a-fors). Both are used to make comparisons that add color and power to ideas. An example of a simile is She has a mind like a computer. In this simile, a person's mind is compared to a computer. A simile always uses the words *like, as,* or *than* to make a comparison. The metaphor, on the other hand, makes a direct comparison: Her mind is a computer.

Vocabulary in Context. How accurate are you in using words you think you already know? Do you know that the word *exotic* means "a thing or person from a foreign country?" So, exotic flowers and exotic costumes are flowers and costumes from foreign countries. *Exotic* has been used incorrectly so often and for so long that it has developed a second meaning. Most people use *exotic* to mean "strikingly unusual, as in color or design."

Many people think that the words *imply* and *infer* mean the same thing. They do not. A writer may imply, or suggest, something. The reader then infers what the writer implied. In other words, to imply is to "suggest an idea." To infer is to "take meaning out."

It is easy to see what would happen to a passage if a reader skipped a word or two that he or she did not know and imposed fuzzy meanings on a few others. The result would inevitably be a gross misunderstanding of the writer's message. You will become a better reader if you learn the exact meanings and different shades of meaning of the words that are already familiar to you.

In this book, you should be able to figure out the meanings of many words from their context—that is, from the words and phrases around them. If this method does not work for you, however, you may consult a dictionary.

Answering the Main Idea Question

The main idea questions in this book are not the usual multiple-choice variety from which you must select the one correct statement. Rather, you are given three statements and are asked to select the statement that expresses the main idea of the passage, the statement that is too narrow, and the statement that is too broad. You have to work hard and actively to identify all three statements correctly. This new type of question teaches you to recognize the differences among statements that, at first, seem almost equal.

To help you handle these questions, let's go behind the scenes to see how the main idea questions in this book were constructed. The true main idea statement was always written first. It had to be neat, succinct, and positive. The main idea tells who or what the subject of the passage is. It also answers the question Does what? or Is what? Next, keeping the main idea statement in mind, the other two statements were written. They are variations of the main idea statement. The "too narrow" statement had to be in line with the main idea but express only part of it. Likewise, the "too broad" statement had to be in line with the main idea but be too general in scope.

Read the social studies passage below. Then, to learn how to answer the main idea questions, follow the instructions in the box. The answer to each part of the question has been filled in for you. The score for each answer has also been marked.

The Children's Crusade

The Fifth Crusade will live in history. It is truly an unforgettable tragedy. This Crusade was better known as the Children's Crusade. It took place in 1212 and burned itself into the hearts, minds, memories, and imaginations of almost all the people in Europe. People felt bad about it for many years afterward. The reason for the long, lingering remorse might be this. Why did the parents let their children go? The Holy Land was a thousand miles away. It was held by hard-fighting Muslims. Did the parents not foresee life-and-death hardships? Did they think some magic carpet would whisk their children to the Holy Land?

This crusade was made up of young boys and girls. Many of the children were less than 12 years old. There were two armies. One army was from France—the other was from Germany. Neither reached the Holy Land. Almost no children ever returned to their homes.

What happened to most of the children? Many died of hunger. Many died of cold weather. Fatigue took its toll, as did disease. It is a long march to the Mediterranean Sea. Some marchers did reach the sea, but it was stormy. Most children were drowned in overloaded ships. Some reached the shore of Africa, but they were captured and sold as slaves.

	Answer	Score
Mark the *main idea*	M	15
Mark the statement that is *too broad*	B	5
Mark the statement that is *too narrow*	N	5

a. The Children's Crusade led to the tragic death of many children. [M] 15

[This statement gathers all the important points. It gives a correct picture of the main idea in a brief way: (1) Children's Crusade, (2) many children, and (3) tragic deaths.]

b. Many children in the Crusade were less than 12 years old. [N] 5

[This statement is correct, but it is too narrow. Only part of the main idea is included. Mention of the children's deaths is left out.]

c. The death of young boys and girls is sad and unforgettable. [B] 5

[This statement is too broad. It mentions children's deaths, but it does not focus on the specific deaths that are the subject of the passage: those in the Children's Crusade.]

Getting the Most Out of This Book

The following steps could be called "tricks of the trade." Your teachers might call them "rules for learning." It doesn't matter what they are called. What does matter is that they work.

Think about the title. A famous language expert proposes the following "trick" to use when reading. "The first thing to do is to read the title. Then spend a few moments thinking about it."

Writers spend much time thinking up good titles. They try to pack a lot of meaning into them. It makes sense, then, for you to spend a few seconds trying to dig out some meaning. These few moments of thought will give you a head start on a passage.

Thinking about the title can help you in another way too. It helps you concentrate on a passage before you begin reading. Why does this happen? Thinking about the title fills your head with thoughts about the passage. There's no room for anything else to get in to break your concentration.

The Dot Step. Here is a method that will speed up your reading. It also builds comprehension at the same time.

Spend a few moments with the title. Then read quickly through the passage. Next, without looking back, answer the six questions by placing a dot in the box next to each answer of your choice. The dots will be your "unofficial" answers. For the main idea question (question 1) place your dot in the box next to the statement that you think is the main idea.

The dot system helps by making you think hard on your first, fast reading. The practice you gain by trying to grasp and remember ideas makes you a stronger reader.

The Checkmark Step. First, answer the main idea question. Follow the steps that are given above each set of statements for this question. Use a capital letter to mark your final answer to each part of the main idea question.

You have answered the other five questions with a dot. Now read the passage once more carefully. This time, mark your final answer to each question by placing a checkmark (√) in the box next to the answer of your choice. The answers with the checkmarks are the ones that will count toward your score.

The Diagnostic Chart. Now move your final answers to the Diagnostic Chart for the passage. These charts start on page 209.

Use the row of boxes beside Passage 1 for the answers to the first passage. Use the row of boxes beside Passage 2 for the answers to the second passage, and so on. Write the letter of your answer to the left of the dotted line in each block.

Correct your answers using the Answer Keys on pages 204–207. When scoring your answers, do not use an *x* for incorrect or a *c* for correct. Instead, use this method: If your choice is incorrect, write the letter of the correct answer to the right of the dotted line in the block.

Thus, the row of answers for each passage will show your incorrect answers. And it will also show the correct answers.

Your Total Comprehension Score. Go back to the passage you have just read. If you answered a question incorrectly, draw a line under the correct choice on the question page. Then write your score for each question on the line provided. Add the scores to get your total comprehension score. Enter that number in the box marked Total Score.

Graphing Your Progress. After you have found your total comprehension score, turn to the Progress Graphs that begin on page 214. Write your score in the box under the number of the passage. Then put an *x* along the line above the box to show your total comprehension score. Join the *x*'s as you go. This will plot a line showing your progress.

Taking Corrective Action. Your incorrect answers give you a way to teach yourself how to read better. Take the time to study these answers.

Go back to the questions. For each question you got wrong, read the correct answer (the one you have underlined) several times. With the correct answer in mind, go back to the passage itself. Read to see why the given answer is better. Try to see where you made your mistake. Try to figure out why you chose an incorrect answer.

The Steps in a Nutshell

Here's a quick review of the steps to follow. Following these steps is the way to get the most out of this book. Be sure you have read and understood everything in this To the Student section before you begin.

1. **Think about the title of the passage.** Try to get all the meaning the writer put into it.
2. **Read the passage quickly.**
3. **Answer the questions, using the dot system.** Use dots to mark your unofficial answers. Don't look back at the passage.
4. **Read the passage again—carefully.**
5. **Mark your final answers.** Put a checkmark (√) in the box to note your final answer. Use capital letters for each part of the main idea question.
6. **Mark your answers on the diagnostic chart.** Record your final answers on the diagnostic chart for the passage. Write your answers to the left of the dotted line in the answer blocks for the passage.
7. **Correct your answers.** Use the answer keys on pages 204–207. If an answer is not correct, write the correct answer in the right side of the

block, beside your incorrect answer. Then go back to the question page. Place a line under the correct answer.

8. **Find your total comprehension score.** Find this by adding up the points you earned for each question. Enter the total in the box marked Total Score.

9. **Graph your progress.** Enter and plot your score on the progress graph for that passage.

10. **Take corrective action.** Read your wrong answers. Read the passage once more. Try to figure out why you were wrong.

To the Teacher

The Reading Passages

Each of the 100 passages included in this book is related to one of four general content areas: the humanities, social studies, science, or mathematics. Each of these areas has several subcategories; humanities, for example, includes passages that deal with literature, music, art, and architecture. The graphic accompanying the title of each piece identifies the general content area to which it belongs.

In addition, each piece had to meet the following two criteria: high interest level and appropriate readability level.

The high interest level was assured by choosing passages of mature content that would appeal to a wide range of readers. In essence, students read passages that will convey interesting information in a content area, whether that area is the student's chosen field of study or not.

The readability level of each passage was computed by applying Dr. Edward B. Fry's *Formula for Estimating Readability*, thus enabling the arrangement of passages according to grade levels within the book. *Six-Way Paragraphs in the Content Areas, Introductory Level* contains passages that range from reading level 4 to reading level 7, with 25 passages on each level. *Six-Way Paragraphs in the Content Areas, Middle Level* contains passages that range from reading level 7 to reading level 10, with 25 passages on each reading level. The passages in *Six-Way Paragraphs in the Content Areas, Advanced Level* range from reading level 10 to reading level 12[+], with 25 passages on each reading level.

The Six Questions

This book is organized around six essential questions. The most important of these is the main idea question, which is actually a set of three statements. Students must first choose and label the statement that expresses the main idea of the passage; then they must label each of the other statements as being either too narrow or too broad to be the main idea.

In addition to the main idea question, there are five other questions. These questions are within the framework of the following five categories: subject matter, supporting details, conclusion, clarifying devices, and vocabulary in context.

By repeated practice with answering the questions within these six categories, students will develop an active, searching attitude about what they read. These six types of questions will help them become aware of what they are reading at the time they are actually seeing the words and phrases on a page. This type of thinking-while-reading sets the stage for higher comprehension and better retention.

The Diagnostic Chart

The Diagnostic Chart provides the most dignified form of guidance yet devised. With this chart, no one has to point out a student's weaknesses. The chart does that automatically, yielding the information directly and personally to the student, making self-teaching possible. The organization of the questions and the format for marking answers on the chart are what make it work so well.

The six questions for each passage are always in the same order. For example, the question designed to teach the skill of drawing conclusions is always the fourth question, and the main idea question is always first. Keeping the questions in order sets the stage for the smooth working of the chart.

The chart works automatically when students write the letter of their answer choices for each passage in the spaces provided. Even after completing only one passage, the chart will reveal the type or types of questions answered correctly, as well as the types answered incorrectly. As the answers for more passages are recorded, the chart will show the types of questions that are missed consistently. A pattern can be seen after three or more passages have been completed. For example, if a student answers question 4 (drawing conclusions) incorrectly for three out of four passages, the student's weakness in this area shows up automatically.

Once a weakness is revealed, have your students take the following steps: First, turn to the instructional pages in the beginning of the book and study the section in which the topic is discussed. Second, go back and reread the questions that were missed in that particular category. Then, with the correct answer to a question in mind, read the entire passage again, trying to see how the writer developed the answer to the question. Do this for each question that was missed. Third, when reading future passages, make an extra effort to correctly answer the questions in that particular category. Fourth, if the difficulty continues, arrange to see your teacher.

Each of the 100 passages included in this book is related to one of four general content areas: humanities, social studies, science, or mathematics. The graphic accompanying the title of each piece identifies the general content area to which it belongs.

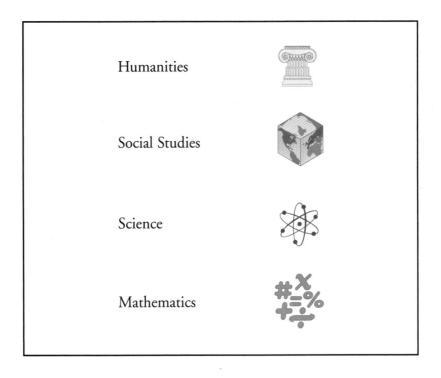

Humanities

Social Studies

Science

Mathematics

1 Matter

Matter is all around you. Matter is the substance that makes all things. Scientists define matter as anything that has weight and takes up space. Is it possible to prove that the things you see around you are made of matter? Actually, such a proof just requires that you use a little common sense.

First, does each item have weight? Scientists use a scale to prove whether something has weight. A book, for example, might weigh one pound. A person might weigh 125 pounds. A sandwich might weigh only six ounces. If we put any of these items on a scale, we can find how much they weigh. Therefore, all of them have a specific weight.

Second, let's prove that the things you see take up space. For example, a book lying on a desk takes up space on the surface of the desk. A person sitting on a chair fills space in the chair. A sandwich in a plastic bag fills space in the bag. Once you know that a book, a person, and a sandwich have weight and take up space, you can see that they all are made of matter.

What about things that you can't see, such as air? Air is difficult to weigh on a scale. But you know that something that is heavy can move lighter things out of its way. Air moves the leaves on plants and the hairs on our head, so we can conclude that air has weight. It's also true that if you blow air into a balloon, the air fills space inside the balloon. Since air has weight and takes up space, it is clear that it is made of matter.

Not everything, however, is made of matter. For example, you might have a million things on your mind. Those things, however, are <u>abstract</u> thoughts and ideas. Thoughts and ideas are items that neither have weight nor take up space. Thus they are not made of matter.

Main Idea	1		
		Answer	**Score**
	Mark the *main idea*	M	15
	Mark the statement that is *too broad*	B	5
	Mark the statement that is *too narrow*	N	5
	a. Matter has weight and takes up space.	☐	____
	b. Matter is in everything.	☐	____
	c. A sandwich is made of matter.	☐	____

Score 15 points for each correct answer.   Score

Subject Matter   **2**   This passage is mainly about
☐ a. how to show if something is made of matter.
☐ b. how scientists measure the weight of matter.
☐ c. how scientists measure the space of matter.
☐ d. types of matter that we cannot see.   _____

Supporting Details   **3**   A characteristic of all matter is that it
☐ a. can be seen.
☐ b. occupies the mind.
☐ c. can be eaten.
☐ d. occupies space.   _____

Conclusion   **4**   The final paragraph suggests that to be sure something is matter, you must
☐ a. evaluate your thoughts and ideas.
☐ b. clear your mind of your worries.
☐ c. prove that it has weight and takes up space.
☐ d. be able to see and touch it.   _____

Clarifying Devices   **5**   The author orders the ideas in the passage by using
☐ a. a spatial description.
☐ b. time order.
☐ c. cause and effect.
☐ d. signal words such as *First* and *Second*.   _____

Vocabulary in Context   **6**   An example of something <u>abstract</u> is a
☐ a. dream.
☐ b. window.
☐ c. feather.
☐ d. thread.   _____

Add your scores for questions 1–6. Enter the total here and on the graph on page 214.   Total Score   _____

3

2 Orchestra Basics

They often play classical music. They also play marches, tangos, and waltzes. Maybe their music excites you. Maybe it bores you. But orchestras are a basic part of music tradition.

An orchestra is made up of four groups of instruments. The largest group is the strings. One well-known stringed instrument is the violin. An orchestra has many of these. Often 15 or 20 are being played at once. Other stringed instruments are violas, cellos, and basses. A viola looks like a violin, but it has a lower sound. Cellos and basses are larger. They rest on the floor. They are played with a bow. Sometimes a harp is also played. The string section sits at the front of the orchestra. It is at the right, left, and front of the conductor.

Another section is the woodwinds. It includes several instruments. Clarinets, flutes, and oboes are woodwinds. A bassoon is another. It has a deep tone. How did these instruments get their name? At one time, they were all made from wood. (Now some, such as flutes, are made from metal.) And players blow into them, using "wind." Woodwind players sit in front of the conductor. They are right behind the strings.

Brass is a third section. In it are various kinds of horns. Three or four may be trumpets. There may also be trombones and French horns. (A French horn has a long tube coiled in a circle. It makes a <u>mellow</u> sound.) The tuba is also in the brass section. It is the largest brass instrument. The brass section sits right behind the woodwinds.

The final section is percussion. It includes any instrument that is struck. An orchestra may have several kinds of drums. Bells are also percussion instruments. So are xylophones and pianos. Most of these instruments are loud, so they are put at the back of the orchestra.

Main Idea	1	Answer	Score
	Mark the *main idea*	**M**	**15**
	Mark the statement that is *too broad*	**B**	**5**
	Mark the statement that is *too narrow*	**N**	**5**

    a. Orchestras include many kinds of woodwind instruments. ☐ _____

    b. Orchestras are made up of four different groups of instruments. ☐ _____

    c. Orchestras play beautiful music. ☐ _____

4

Score 15 points for each correct answer.   **Score**

Subject Matter   **2**   This passage is mainly about
        ☐ a. the music played by orchestras.
        ☐ b. the instruments in an orchestra's four sections.
        ☐ c. what different instruments sound like.
        ☐ d. where different sections of an orchestra sit.   _____

Supporting   **3**   The largest section in an orchestra is the
Details
        ☐ a. strings.
        ☐ b. brass.
        ☐ c. woodwinds.
        ☐ d. percussion.   _____

Conclusion   **4**   A xylophone would be found in the
        ☐ a. woodwind section.
        ☐ b. brass section.
        ☐ c. percussion section.
        ☐ d. string section.   _____

Clarifying   **5**   To help you visualize an orchestra, the writer explains
Devices
        ☐ a. how various instruments sound.
        ☐ b. where different sections sit.
        ☐ c. why pianos are percussion instruments.
        ☐ d. the difference between a violin and a viola.   _____

Vocabulary   **6**   In this passage the word <u>mellow</u> means
in Context
        ☐ a. out of touch.
        ☐ b. drumlike.
        ☐ c. musical.
        ☐ d. smooth and pleasing to the ear.   _____

Add your scores for questions 1–6. Enter the total here   **Total**
and on the graph on page 214.   **Score**   _____

3 Getting Help with Math

It's nine o'clock on a Tuesday night. You are trying to finish your math assignment. You have only two problems left to go. Almost done! You are looking forward to a nice snack and your favorite TV show. You read the next problem and groan. You don't have a clue how to do it. You may check your notes from class. Or you may try reading your textbook. But the problem might as well be written in a foreign language.

Does this sound familiar? Most people who have taken any kind of math class have had this experience. What do you do when you get stuck? Perhaps you call a friend. Or you ask a family member for help. But what if it's late at night?

Years ago there were very few ways to get help if you were stuck on a math problem. Math is different from other school subjects. You often cannot find what to do in a book. A dictionary or even an encyclopedia probably won't help you. You need someone to show you the steps. Learning most kinds of math is something like learning to play a musical instrument. You need a <u>coach</u> to show you what to do.

In many areas there are homework telephone lines. These hot lines have volunteers. They can help you do homework in all subjects. A math volunteer can explain the steps in a math problem that has you stumped.

Today you can also get help on the Internet. There are several homework help programs and Web pages. In some, you leave your question on a message board. Or you write it in an e-mail note. In other math help programs there are live volunteer teachers. You can wait for a real math teacher to help you do the problem.

Main Idea	1		Answer	Score
	Mark the *main idea*		M	15
	Mark the statement that is *too broad*		B	5
	Mark the statement that is *too narrow*		N	5

    a. Dictionaries and encyclopedias won't help you do math homework. ☐ _____

    b. There are various ways to get help if you have trouble with math homework. ☐ _____

    c. A lot of students find it hard to do math. ☐ _____

Score 15 points for each correct answer.   **Score**

Subject Matter   2   This passage is mostly concerned with
     ☐ a. why math is difficult to do.
     ☐ b. ways of getting help with math homework.
     ☐ c. using reference books to do math homework.
     ☐ d. using a computer to do math.   _____

Supporting   3   In the first paragraph, the writer asks you to
Details   ☐ a. solve a math problem.
     ☐ b. recall how you once asked someone to
        help you with math.
     ☐ c. use a computer to get help in math homework.
     ☐ d. imagine yourself doing math homework. _____

Conclusion   4   The passage suggests that people who need math
     homework help should
     ☐ a. not take any more math classes.
     ☐ b. try a homework help program on the Internet.
     ☐ c. watch some television.
     ☐ d. write an e-mail note to a friend.   _____

Clarifying   5   The writer compares learning math to
Devices   ☐ a. learning to play a musical instrument.
     ☐ b. using a computer.
     ☐ c. finishing a homework assignment.
     ☐ d. calling a friend to get help on homework. _____

Vocabulary   6   In this passage the word <u>coach</u> means
in Context   ☐ a. someone who teaches a sport.
     ☐ b. someone who can explain math problems.
     ☐ c. someone who will solve problems for you.
     ☐ d. the head of an Internet Web site. _____

Add your scores for questions 1–6. Enter the total here **Total**
and on the graph on page 214.   **Score** _____

4 History: What It Is, What It Means

Do you know what history is? Here is one answer. It is everything humans have done and thought. Here is a more specific answer. History is the story of events. It is the story of nations and persons. How people began writing is part of history. So is the Hundred Years' War. So is the first airplane flight. So is last year's election.

How do we know about the past? There are many sources. Some are oral. Some are visual or written. We can learn of the past from one person's memory. We can learn from stories handed down through generations. We can see the past in a piece of Stone Age flint. We see it in old paintings and photos. We read about the past in old records. They may be ships' logs or church records. They may be diaries of pioneers. They may be journals of presidents. Each fact and story is interesting. Each is important. Each is part of history.

It is impossible to record everything about an event or person. Facts must be carefully chosen to tell what happened. Questions have to be asked. Answers must be found. Different accounts of a single event need to be put together.

This is the job of historians. They try to come up with an <u>accurate</u> story. They look carefully at what they find. Then they put the past together again. Historians search for causes of events. They also look for history's effects. Sometimes they do not know how or why something happened. Then they come up with theories. These theories are based on the facts. They may help explain certain events.

When the facts are put together, a story of events and nations comes forth. The story of humans can be told.

Main Idea 1

	Answer	Score
Mark the *main idea*	M	15
Mark the statement that is *too broad*	B	5
Mark the statement that is *too narrow*	N	5

a. History is the Hundred Years' War and the first airplane flight. ☐ _____

b. To understand history, facts must be studied and analyzed. ☐ _____

c. History is all about the past. ☐ _____

Score 15 points for each correct answer.   **Score**

Subject Matter   **2**   Another good title for this passage is
    ☐ a. A History of the World.
    ☐ b. The Story of Nations.
    ☐ c. How to Become a Historian.
    ☐ d. Making Sense of History.   _____

Supporting   **3**   Which of the following is an example of a
Details   visual history source?
    ☐ a. an old photograph
    ☐ b. a diary
    ☐ c. a person's memory
    ☐ d. stories   _____

Conclusion   **4**   To be a good historian, a person must **not**
    ☐ a. want to know about the past.
    ☐ b. be in a hurry.
    ☐ c. be able to analyze information.
    ☐ d. read a lot.   _____

Clarifying   **5**   The question in the second paragraph alerts the
Devices   reader that the sentences that follow will
    ☐ a. list some sources of historical information.
    ☐ b. tell why there is no information about
        the past.
    ☐ c. tell why history confuses the writer.
    ☐ d. give reasons why history is important.   _____

Vocabulary   **6**   The word <u>accurate</u> means
in Context
    ☐ a. mistaken.
    ☐ b. agreeable.
    ☐ c. believable.
    ☐ d. correct.   _____

Add your scores for questions 1–6. Enter the total here   **Total**
and on the graph on page 214.   **Score**   _____

5 Elements of Fiction

Do you like to read short stories or novels? Made-up stories like these are called fiction. Good fiction sounds as if it really happened. (Or at least it sounds as if it *could* happen.) The writer may use events from his or her own life. But they are put together in a way that is not true.

Fictional stories have three basic elements. They are setting, character, and plot.

Setting is when and where a story happens. Many popular novels are set in the present. But some go back—or forward—in time. Westerns are often set in the 1800s. Books about King Arthur are set in <u>medieval</u> times. Science fiction may have a future setting. The place of a story can vary too. It may be anywhere from New York to the jungles of Asia to Mars. A long novel may have several settings.

Characters are the people in a story. Most stories have only one or two main characters. (This is true even of long stories.) The writer may tell us what they look like. We also learn about them from how they act. What other characters say about them can help too. Of course, we learn more about main characters than minor ones. If we like the characters, we usually like the story. We want to find out what happens to these people.

Plot is what happens in the story. Usually the main character must deal with a conflict. It may be with another character. (Two brothers are competing in business.) Or it may be because of worries or fears. (A woman is afraid to leave her house.) By the end of the story, the conflict is solved. The main character may have learned something. But the ending may not be happy. A marriage may end. Someone may die. Was the story good anyway? That decision is left for the reader to make.

Main Idea	1		
		Answer	**Score**
	Mark the *main idea*	M	15
	Mark the statement that is *too broad*	B	5
	Mark the statement that is *too narrow*	N	5

a. The basic parts of fiction are plot, character, and setting. ☐ _____

b. There are various ways to learn about characters in a story. ☐ _____

c. Short stories and novels are called fiction. ☐ _____

Subject Matter   **2**   This passage is mainly about
- ☐ a. elements that are part of every fictional story.
- ☐ b. why people enjoy reading fiction.
- ☐ c. characteristics of science fiction.
- ☐ d. differences between novels and short stories.   _____

Supporting Details   **3**   The setting in fiction includes
- ☐ a. time, place, and characters.
- ☐ b. time and place.
- ☐ c. the things that happen.
- ☐ d. reasons for the conflict.   _____

Conclusion   **4**   Conflict in a story can be the result of
- ☐ a. the length of the story.
- ☐ b. the writer's use of description.
- ☐ c. an unhappy ending.
- ☐ d. things in a character's mind as well as things that are outside.   _____

Clarifying Devices   **5**   The writer has organized this passage
- ☐ a. by defining and explaining three terms.
- ☐ b. in chronological order.
- ☐ c. by telling about several famous novels.
- ☐ d. by describing possible story settings.   _____

Vocabulary in Context   **6**   The word <u>medieval</u> means
- ☐ a. in the future.
- ☐ b. very beautiful.
- ☐ c. in the Middle Ages.
- ☐ d. hard to hear.   _____

Add your scores for questions 1–6. Enter the total here and on the graph on page 214.   **Total Score**   _____

6 Visualizing Percents

Many people find percents difficult. A percent is very different from a number such as 25. You can easily imagine 25 golf balls. Or you might think of 25 dollars or 25 feet. Twenty-five of something is easy to visualize. You can picture it in your mind.

It is harder to form a mental picture of 25 percent. That is because a percent compares things. It compares the number to 100. Think of the percent sign (%) as meaning "out of 100." Thus 25 percent means "25 out of 100." This may help you understand what 25 percent means. But it doesn't help you make a mental picture of 25 percent.

To picture 25 percent, you need an example. That is because 25 percent can mean different things. Getting 25 percent of a small number is different from getting 25 percent of a large number. For example, 25 percent of $83 is much less than 25 percent of $8,300.

Is there a way to picture an example like 25 percent of $83? One way is to sketch two bars, both of the same length. One bar, the percent bar, has 100 units. The other, the number bar, has 83 units.

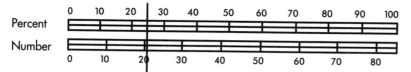

Notice that the sketch has a <u>vertical</u> line. This line goes through 25 on the percent bar and hits the number bar at about 21. So the diagram helps you "see" a percent. It shows that 25 percent of $83 is about $21.

Making bar diagrams for percents can assist you in comprehending what the percents mean. Your diagrams need not be beautiful; in fact, they can be very rough. They are also a useful way to doublecheck answers you arrive at with a calculator.

Main Idea	1		
		Answer	**Score**
	Mark the *main idea*	M	15
	Mark the statement that is *too broad*	B	5
	Mark the statement that is *too narrow*	N	5

a. A bar diagram can help you if you have trouble picturing percents. ☐ _____

b. Solving problems with percents is a useful skill. ☐ _____

c. Twenty-five percent of 83 is about 21. ☐ _____

Subject Matter   **2**   This passage is mainly about
- ☐ a. doing percent problems in your head.
- ☐ b. using a calculator for percent problems.
- ☐ c. estimating percents with diagrams.
- ☐ d. finding percents of large numbers.   _____

Supporting Details   **3**   If you draw a percent diagram, the two bars in it must be
- ☐ a. four inches long.
- ☐ b. divided into 10 equal parts.
- ☐ c. drawn on graph paper.
- ☐ d. the same length.   _____

Conclusion   **4**   The first three paragraphs explain why
- ☐ a. percents are not numbers.
- ☐ b. it is difficult to make mental pictures of percents.
- ☐ c. 25 percent of $83 is about $21.
- ☐ d. 25 golf balls is different from 25 dollars.   _____

Clarifying Devices   **5**   A percent diagram would **not** help you
- ☐ a. to estimate an answer to a percent problem.
- ☐ b. to check an answer to a percent problem.
- ☐ c. to avoid making errors in percent problems.
- ☐ d. if you didn't know what *percent* means.   _____

Vocabulary in Context   **6**   The word <u>vertical</u> means
- ☐ a. from side to side.
- ☐ b. diagonal.
- ☐ c. up and down.
- ☐ d. made up of several small pieces.   _____

Add your scores for questions 1–6. Enter the total here and on the graph on page 214.   **Total Score**   _____

7 The Common Cold

Got the sniffles? You're not alone. The common cold will strike in the United States more than 61 million times this year. That's a lot of stuffy noses, sore throats, and coughs. You'd think scientists would have found a cure by now. For being so common, however, a cold is quite complex.

A cold is caused by a virus. And it's not just one type of virus. More than 200 viruses cause colds. A cold virus attacks healthy cells of the nose, throat, or lungs. The virus gets into the cells and takes control. A single virus makes hundreds or thousands of cold viruses inside each cell. Eventually, the cell bursts open and dies. The viruses, though, escape and attack other healthy cells. By now you're sneezing and coughing. Your throat is sore. The viruses keep infecting your healthy cells.

Only your body can fight cold viruses. Billions of white blood cells travel in the blood. White blood cells make <u>antibodies</u>. These proteins attach themselves to viruses and destroy them. It's a slow process. Killing the viruses takes one to two weeks.

What can you do to fight a cold? There isn't much you can do. Antibiotic drugs don't work against viruses. Nose drops and cough medicines only relieve symptoms. Chicken soup seems to help. Vitamin C may help too. A dose of 1,000 milligrams of Vitamin C on the first day of a cold may quicken your recovery.

Be healthy and you may not catch a cold at all. Eat a well-balanced diet and get eight hours of sleep each day. Exercise regularly. The cold virus spreads through the air, so stay away from coughing, sneezing people. Also, the cold virus can live up to three hours outside the body. That means you can pick it up from touching money, doorknobs, and other people. So wash your hands often. Prevention is the best action!

Main Idea	1		Answer	Score
	Mark the *main idea*		M	15
	Mark the statement that is *too broad*		B	5
	Mark the statement that is *too narrow*		N	5
	a. A cold is a very common illness.		☐	_____
	b. The common cold is caused by a virus that antibodies will finally kill.		☐	_____
	c. More than 200 viruses can cause the common cold.		☐	_____

Subject Matter **2** This passage is mainly concerned with
- ☐ a. antibodies.
- ☐ b. viruses.
- ☐ c. antibiotics.
- ☐ d. common colds.   _____

Supporting Details **3** The common cold is started by
- ☐ a. a low white-blood cell count.
- ☐ b. a virus.
- ☐ c. a poor diet.
- ☐ d. shaking hands with other people.   _____

Conclusion **4** We can conclude from this passage that the common cold
- ☐ a. will be curable in the near future.
- ☐ b. causes fatigue and watery eyes.
- ☐ c. is something people just have to live with.
- ☐ d. can be prevented with nose drops.   _____

Clarifying Devices **5** In the second and third paragraphs, the author explains the workings of a cold virus through
- ☐ a. a step-by-step explanation.
- ☐ b. scientific studies.
- ☐ c. detailed word pictures.
- ☐ d. a list of symptoms.   _____

Vocabulary in Context **6** <u>Antibodies</u> are
- ☐ a. proteins that attack viruses.
- ☐ b. white blood cells.
- ☐ c. drugs that fight viruses.
- ☐ d. vitamins.   _____

Add your scores for questions 1–6. Enter the total here and on the graph on page 214.   **Total Score**   _____

15

8 The Roman Army

The Roman Empire was a great power in ancient times. But the first Roman army was made up of ordinary citizens. Young men did the fighting. Older men cleaned weapons and defended their cities. They served only in crisis or war. Then the time came when Rome needed well-trained men. A new army of full-time, paid soldiers was created. The men were called legionaries. Legionaries stayed in the army for 20 years. They trained, fought, and built roads and bridges. The legionaries served in groups called legions. Each legion was made up of about 6,000 men. At the height of the Roman Empire, around 27 B.C., 28 legions served the empire.

Legionaries carried their weapons, clothes, tents, food, and cooking pots. They marched about 21 miles a day. When they came to a river, they built a bridge. Each night they set up camp. They built earth walls to protect the camp from attack. They also built roads so the army could march between towns and camps. About 50,000 miles of highways were built. They connected all parts of the Roman Empire. (Pieces of some of these roads still exist today.)

Sometimes the Roman army attacked towns. A town might have walls made of thick stone. Its gate would be heavy and wooden. The town's soldiers defended the town by standing on top of the walls to hurl spears and shoot arrows. The attacking Roman soldiers used a movable tower. They pushed the tower toward the enemy's walls. They lowered a drawbridge from the tower to the top of the wall. Then the Roman soldiers swarmed across the drawbridge to capture the town.

At their peak, no one equaled the Romans, their army, or their empire. They had no <u>rivals</u>.

Main Idea	1		
		Answer	**Score**
	Mark the *main idea*	M	15
	Mark the statement that is *too broad*	B	5
	Mark the statement that is *too narrow*	N	5
	a. The Romans had a very large empire.	☐	_____
	b. The Roman army was an important part of the Roman Empire.	☐	_____
	c. The Roman legions sometimes attacked heavily defended towns.	☐	_____

Score 15 points for each correct answer. Score

Subject Matter   **2**   This passage is mostly about
- ☐ a. what the Roman legions did.
- ☐ b. who trained Roman soldiers.
- ☐ c. why Roman roads survive to this day.
- ☐ d. the Roman army before the legions were formed.   _____

Supporting Details   **3**   The legionaries carried
- ☐ a. road maps.
- ☐ b. a drawbridge.
- ☐ c. their tents.
- ☐ d. movable towers.   _____

Conclusion   **4**   Which adjective best describes the Roman army?
- ☐ a. vicious
- ☐ b. well-trained
- ☐ c. weak
- ☐ d. small   _____

Clarifying Devices   **5**   The date 27 B.C. in the first paragraph refers to
- ☐ a. the first year that Rome had a full-time army.
- ☐ b. the year that 50,000 miles of roads were built.
- ☐ c. the year the Roman army invented movable towers.
- ☐ d. the time when the Roman Empire was largest and most powerful.   _____

Vocabulary in Context   **6**   In this passage the word <u>rivals</u> means
- ☐ a. equals.
- ☐ b. crimes.
- ☐ c. leaders.
- ☐ d. friends.   _____

Add your scores for questions 1–6. Enter the total here and on the graph on page 214.   Total Score   _____

9 Are We There Yet?

If you are like most people, you have probably been lost on a car trip. You may stop and ask directions, but sometimes the directions aren't helpful. Sometimes they may even be wrong! The best way to not get lost is to learn to use road maps.

The first thing to understand about road maps is the scale. The scale on a map tells you how the map relates to the actual area it is showing. For example, you may see a note on a map saying "1 in. = 150 miles." On this map, each inch stands for 150 miles. A distance of 10 inches equals 1,500 miles (10 times 150 = 1,500). If the map is 20 inches wide, it could show the whole United States.

A map with the scale 1 in. = 150 miles can help you plan a car trip from Boston to Los Angeles, but it will not help you find your way around city streets. For this you need a city street map. The scale on this map will be different. For instance, every inch may show one half of a mile. A map isn't useful if it doesn't have the right scale for your trip.

The second tip for using road maps is finding two locations. You need to know where you are right now and where you want to go. Then select the roads or streets you will use to get there. Use the <u>intersections</u> of large streets or highways to help you zero in on locations.

Finally, it is an excellent idea to keep a small compass in your car. The compass will tell you if you are driving north, south, or some other direction. On most road maps, north is at the top. Turn the map so the top edge is towards north. This can help you avoid driving in the opposite direction.

It may take some practice to learn to use road maps. But it's worth it. If you have a map with the right scale and know how to use it, you will never get lost again.

Main Idea	1		
		Answer	Score
	Mark the *main idea*	M	15
	Mark the statement that is *too broad*	B	5
	Mark the statement that is *too narrow*	N	5

a. A map scale shows how distances on the map are related to real distances. ☐ _____

b. Road maps give useful information. ☐ _____

c. Using a road map will help you not get lost on a car trip. ☐ _____

Score 15 points for each correct answer.   **Score**

Subject Matter   **2**   Another good title for this passage would be
       ☐ a. Finding the Distance Between Two Cities.
       ☐ b. Learning to Use Road Maps.
       ☐ c. Understanding How a Compass Works.
       ☐ d. Estimating Costs for a Car Trip.   _____

Supporting   **3**   On a map with a scale of 1 in. = 150 miles,
Details   10 inches represents
       ☐ a. 15 miles.
       ☐ b. 150 miles.
       ☐ c. 1,500 miles.
       ☐ d. 15,000 miles.   _____

Conclusion   **4**   A road map won't help you on a trip if you
       ☐ a. don't know where you are to begin with.
       ☐ b. don't have a compass.
       ☐ c. turn the map so the top edge is north.
       ☐ d. don't know the distance between two locations.   _____

Clarifying   **5**   The writer explains the idea of a map scale by
Devices   ☐ a. describing a diagram.
       ☐ b. giving tips for using a map.
       ☐ c. giving an example.
       ☐ d. telling a story in which people got lost.   _____

Vocabulary   **6**   In this passage the word <u>intersections</u> means
in Context   ☐ a. places where two streets meet.
       ☐ b. two cars crashing into each other.
       ☐ c. lines to help you fold a street map.
       ☐ d. ways to cut maps into smaller sections.   _____

Add your scores for questions 1–6. Enter the total here   **Total**
and on the graph on page 214.   **Score**   _____

10 Kinds of Art

Some paintings you look at and understand right away. You see a picture of a woman. You see a country road. You see a boat on a river. Perhaps the painter is trying to tell you something. Perhaps not. It does not really matter. You can look at the painting and see what it's about. You can simply enjoy the picture.

Paintings like these may be called *realistic*. But some are more realistic than others. For example, the picture of a woman may have soft, blurred edges. A woman does not look *exactly* like that. But still, you recognize her for what she is. Another name for this kind of art is *representational*. You recognize what the painting represents.

Other paintings are more difficult to comprehend. You look at them closely. But you see little that you recognize. Such a painting may be blotches of color. Or it may be filled with tiny squares. Or it may be all one color, with one contrasting stripe painted across it. You look at such paintings and ask yourself, "Am I supposed to see a picture here?"

The answer, usually, is that you are not. There is no picture of a woman hidden in those blotches of color. The artist is not trying to represent anything. Instead, he or she may be experimenting. One artist may be trying to combine colors in new and interesting ways. Another may be looking to create different <u>textures</u> on the canvas. Art of this type is called *abstract*. You may not like all the abstract art you see. But you can still get something out of it. Do you like the colors? Do you like the texture or design? An abstract painting may be different from what you are used to. But you can accept it for what it is.

Main Idea	1	Answer	Score
	Mark the *main idea*	M	15
	Mark the statement that is *too broad*	B	5
	Mark the statement that is *too narrow*	N	5

a. Art is a fascinating subject to study.	☐	_____
b. Some art is realistic; other art is abstract.	☐	_____
c. Some painters experiment with color and design.	☐	_____

Subject Matter   **2**   The purpose of this passage is to
- ☐ a. provide a short history of art.
- ☐ b. explain different techniques for putting paint on a canvas.
- ☐ c. explain differences between realistic and abstract art.
- ☐ d. convince the reader to visit art museums.   _____

Supporting Details   **3**   Representational art is
- ☐ a. abstract.
- ☐ b. realistic.
- ☐ c. modern.
- ☐ d. done only with water colors.   _____

Conclusion   **4**   The writer seems to feel that
- ☐ a. abstract art is ridiculous.
- ☐ b. you should look for pictures in abstract art.
- ☐ c. people can learn to appreciate abstract art.
- ☐ d. pictures of women should not be blurred.   _____

Clarifying Devices   **5**   The writer has organized this passage by
- ☐ a. comparison and contrast.
- ☐ b. order of importance.
- ☐ c. time order.
- ☐ d. spatial order.   _____

Vocabulary in Context   **6**   In this passage the word <u>textures</u> means
- ☐ a. colors and how bright they are.
- ☐ b. designs.
- ☐ c. squares and triangles.
- ☐ d. appearances or feelings of surfaces.   _____

Add your scores for questions 1–6. Enter the total here and on the graph on page 214.   **Total Score**   _____

11 What Is Geography?

Geography is an old area of study. It goes back to early Greece. The Greeks wrote about the natural world. They noted where things were on the earth. The word *geography* comes from the Greeks. It means "earth description."

Geographers today describe the earth. They describe the size of land masses. They study the seas. They collect data on climates. They watch plant and animal life. They also look for connections. Connections mean a lot to them. In fact, connections are <u>foremost</u> in their studies. They try to connect people with the earth.

Geographers look at people and the earth in four ways. First, they think about location. Location means where people and places are. Location tells exactly where something is. It also tells if something is near or far.

Second, they study relationships. They see how places affect people's lives. They figure out why people and things are where they are.

Third, they look at movement. They note how goods and people go from place to place.

Finally, they look at regions. These are areas with names. Regions are named for governments. They are named for languages. They may be named for religious groups. They are sometimes named for ethnic groups. They may also be named for landforms or climate.

Maps and globes are the geographer's tools. Census counts and land surveys are tools too. So are photos and satellites. They tell about remote places.

Geographers study many things. They study climate. They examine land. They look at population. They study economics. They note how one thing affects another. They try to see how people and the earth fit together.

Main Idea	1		
		Answer	**Score**
	Mark the *main idea*	M	15
	Mark the statement that is *too broad*	B	5
	Mark the statement that is *too narrow*	N	5

a. Geographers use tools such as maps and globes. ☐ _____

b. Geography is interesting. ☐ _____

c. Geography is the study of connections between people and the earth. ☐ _____

Score 15 points for each correct answer.   **Score**

Subject Matter **2** This passage explains that geography is
- [ ] a. the study of many aspects of the earth.
- [ ] b. the study of photography and satellites.
- [ ] c. a religious group.
- [ ] d. the study of ancient Greece.   _____

Supporting Details **3** The passage discusses how many ways to look at people and the earth?
- [ ] a. two
- [ ] b. four
- [ ] c. six
- [ ] d. ten   _____

Conclusion **4** For a geographer, the phrase "Spanish-speaking" might identify a
- [ ] a. movement.
- [ ] b. region.
- [ ] c. satellite.
- [ ] d. relationship.   _____

Clarifying Devices **5** In the first paragraph, the phrase "earth description" is used as
- [ ] a. a simile.
- [ ] b. a definition.
- [ ] c. a name for the early Greeks.
- [ ] d. one of several ways of looking at the earth.   _____

Vocabulary in Context **6** The word <u>foremost</u> means
- [ ] a. debated.
- [ ] b. forgotten.
- [ ] c. first.
- [ ] d. fourth.   _____

Add your scores for questions 1–6. Enter the total here and on the graph on page 214.   **Total Score**   _____

12 Water for Life

Heading out for some exercise? You'll take your shoes, socks, and a towel. You might take a music headset. But you'll also need a water bottle. Here is why. When you exercise, you sweat. It's your body's way of cooling down. The more you sweat, the more water your body loses. But exercise also reduces thirst. If you're not thirsty, you may not drink water. You could lose too much water and become <u>dehydrated</u>. A water loss of 10 percent can make you sick. A water loss of 20 percent can kill you. So you need to be careful.

Here's how to keep your body hydrated. About two hours before you exercise, drink one 500-milliliter ($\frac{1}{2}$ liter) bottle of water. Then drink another half bottle right before you begin. Drink water every 20 minutes as you exercise. You'll need water long before you're thirsty.

You need water even when you're not exercising. You should drink about four bottles of water each day. Why so much? Your body cells are mostly water. So is your blood. Water helps your body to digest food and remove wastes. But your body loses water as you breathe, sweat, and urinate. It loses about 2.5 liters (2,500 milliliters) of water each day.

You must replace the water your body loses. You can get water from many sources. Drinking water is the best source. Food and other fluids are good too. All food has some water in it. Fruits and vegetables are high in water. Milk, juices, and other drinks have water. So take your pick. And remember to drink more water when you exercise. A happy body is a hydrated body!

Main Idea 1

	Answer	Score
Mark the *main idea*	M	15
Mark the statement that is *too broad*	B	5
Mark the statement that is *too narrow*	N	5

a. Your body loses about 2.5 liters of water each day. ☐ _____

b. Your body needs water whether you are exercising or not. ☐ _____

c. Water is important for everyone. ☐ _____

Subject Matter   **2**   This passage is mainly about
- ☐ a. the benefits of a regular workout.
- ☐ b. sports equipment to take to the gym.
- ☐ c. why our bodies need water.
- ☐ d. how many milliliters a water bottle holds.   _____

Supporting Details   **3**   Losing 10 percent of your body's water
- ☐ a. will not hurt you during exercise.
- ☐ b. can make you ill.
- ☐ c. can kill you.
- ☐ d. will make your skin feel very cold.   _____

Conclusion   **4**   Each day you should drink
- ☐ a. about 2,500 milliliters of water.
- ☐ b. about 500 milliliters of water.
- ☐ c. as much milk as you can.
- ☐ d. only when you get thirsty.   _____

Clarifying Devices   **5**   The author tells how to keep your body hydrated during exercise by presenting
- ☐ a. a diagram.
- ☐ b. a description of a human blood vessel.
- ☐ c. a series of steps to follow.
- ☐ d. the results of an experiment.   _____

Vocabulary in Context   **6**   To become <u>dehydrated</u> is to
- ☐ a. drink too much water.
- ☐ b. lose more water than you take in.
- ☐ c. exercise at least four days a week.
- ☐ d. cool off after exercising.   _____

Add your scores for questions 1–6. Enter the total here and on the graph on page 214.   **Total Score**   _____

13 Appreciating Poetry

It seems that people have always created poetry. They used it to tell stories about heroes. They used it to pass down family histories. Some early poetry was never written down. Poets would <u>recite</u> their poems for groups of people. Maybe the poems would be put on paper later. Often these poems were very long.

Poetry usually has some distinct qualities. For example, poems are broken into lines. But do you pause at the end of each line? Not necessarily. Usually you keep reading till you get to a period or comma. (This is like reading prose.) And some poems rhyme. Many also have a clear beat, or rhythm. For instance, read this line one poet wrote about her husband: "If ever two were one, then surely we." Can you hear the da-DA, da-DA, da-DA, da-DA, da-DA beat?

Often poets try to paint pictures in words. To do this, they might not even write full sentences. They may write short phrases instead. Use your imagination. Try to see in your mind the pictures a poet is painting.

Many poets also use figures of speech. One poet described love this way. He said it was "*like* a red, red rose." He compared love and a rose using the word *like*. This figure of speech is a simile. What if he said "my love *is* a rose"? Then he would be using a metaphor. This is a comparison that does not use *like* or *as*. What if he said "The wind wrapped its arms around me"? The wind is doing the actions of a person. This is called personification.

Some poems tell stories. Some describe things. Some give you new ways of thinking about things. Don't be afraid of poetry. You can learn to enjoy it.

Main Idea	1	Answer	Score
Mark the *main idea*		M	15
Mark the statement that is *too broad*		B	5
Mark the statement that is *too narrow*		N	5

a. If you learn to understand some of the poet's techniques, you will start to enjoy poetry. ☐ _____

b. Some figures of speech that poets use are similes and metaphors. ☐ _____

c. Poetry is a way of writing that started a long time ago. ☐ _____

Score 15 points for each correct answer.   **Score**

Subject Matter 2 This passage is mostly about
- [ ] a. famous poems.
- [ ] b. helpful things to know about reading poems.
- [ ] c. the history of poetry from the earliest days.
- [ ] d. figures of speech.   _____

Supporting Details 3 A figure of speech in which a thing does the actions of a person is
- [ ] a. a simile.
- [ ] b. a metaphor.
- [ ] c. imagery.
- [ ] d. personification.   _____

Conclusion 4 A characteristic of most poets is that they want to
- [ ] a. paint strong pictures in just a few words.
- [ ] b. make all their lines rhyme.
- [ ] c. not use punctuation.
- [ ] d. write long poems.   _____

Clarifying Devices 5 The writer makes clear some of the devices a poet uses by
- [ ] a. giving examples of them.
- [ ] b. explaining their history.
- [ ] c. listing them in alphabetical order.
- [ ] d. naming several poets who use them.   _____

Vocabulary in Context 6 The word <u>recite</u> means
- [ ] a. read silently.
- [ ] b. play a part.
- [ ] c. say out loud.
- [ ] d. write down.   _____

Add your scores for questions 1–6. Enter the total here and on the graph on page 214.   **Total Score** _____

27

14 Brain Cells

What are you doing right now? Yes, you are reading this page. That also means you're moving your eyes. You're thinking. You're breathing. You're listening. Possibly you're shifting positions. You're also feeling things—this book, your chair, emotions. What lets you do all these things at the same time? Your brain.

Your brain is the control center of your body and mind. Without your brain you can't do anything. Your brain contains more than 100 billion nerve cells. Each nerve cell makes from 1,000 to 10,000 connections with other nerve cells. The nerve cells send <u>impulses</u> back and forth within your brain and to and from every part of your body. After you reach the age of 20, though, your brain cells start to die. This is normal. However, if you suffer a stroke, an illness, or an injury, even more nerve cells die in your brain. When a nerve cell dies, the thousands of connections it made with other nerve cells are lost.

Until recently, scientists believed that the brain did not replace its dead cells. New studies, however, prove otherwise. Scientists have found new nerve cells in a part of the brain called the hippocampus. The hippocampus helps the brain form memories from new experiences.

The discovery of these new nerve cells is not a cure for anything yet. It gives hope, however, of a cure for brain damage from such things as epilepsy, Lou Gehrig's disease, car accidents, and strokes. Someday scientists might be able to use the new cells to replace damaged brain cells. Such a cure, however, may take decades to develop. So in the meantime, use your head—protect it!

Main Idea	1	Answer	Score
	Mark the *main idea*	M	15
	Mark the statement that is *too broad*	B	5
	Mark the statement that is *too narrow*	N	5

		Answer	Score
a.	Nerve cells in the brain begin to die when a person reaches the age of 20.	☐	_____
b.	There are a lot of things going on in the human brain.	☐	_____
c.	The brain is a control center regulating thoughts, feelings, and actions.	☐	_____

Subject Matter   **2**   This passage is mainly about
    □ a. why people should wear bike helmets.
    □ b. the number of activities humans can do
      at the same time.
    □ c. the importance of nerve cells in the brain.
    □ d. the number of connections made between
      nerve cells.   _____

Supporting   **3**   Nerve cells in the brain
Details
    □ a. send messages to every part of the body.
    □ b. make connections only to other cells in
      the brain.
    □ c. can cure Lou Gehrig's disease.
    □ d. are a person's memory.   _____

Conclusion   **4**   The last sentence of the passage suggests that people
    □ a. should use their head by carefully thinking
      through situations.
    □ b. should be careful not to injure their brains.
    □ c. have a skull that provides all the protection
      needed by the brain.
    □ d. should see a quick cure for brain disorders. _____

Clarifying   **5**   The author makes clear what the hippocampus is by
Devices
    □ a. tracing its history.
    □ b. comparing it to other parts of the brain.
    □ c. telling how it got its name.
    □ d. explaining what it does.   _____

Vocabulary   **6**   Nerve <u>impulses</u> are
in Context
    □ a. cures.
    □ b. disorders.
    □ c. memories.
    □ d. messages.   _____

Add your scores for questions 1–6. Enter the total here **Total**
and on the graph on page 214.   **Score** _____

15 The Caves of Lascaux

Imagine looking for your lost dog. You step into a cave. But instead of the dog, you find beautiful cave paintings. You see paintings of horses, deer, and bison. They are drawn in black, brown, red, and yellow. Your first question would probably be "Who did this?"

This is what happened to four French boys in 1940. They found the Lascaux (lahs KOH) caves. The paintings the boys discovered in those caves are 17,000 years old. They were drawn by the prehistoric people called Cro-Magnons.

Cro-Magnons looked much like people of today. They used tools, such as fishing nets, that look familiar too. But their art was <u>extraordinary</u>. The main cave at Lascaux is called the Great Hall of Bulls. It has a picture of bulls and horses in many colors. The largest animal is 18 feet long. There are smaller animals too. They include bison, stags, and a bear. There is also an odd, spotted, two-horned animal.

To the left of the main cave are the most famous paintings. These are drawings of multicolored animals. One painting is called Little Horses. On the ceiling are horses and cows. The most unusual sight may be in the Shaft of the Dead Man. Here is a rhinoceros, a carefully drawn dead man, a wounded bison, and a bird.

Why did Cro-Magnon artists do these beautiful drawings on cave walls? Did the drawings call upon some magical power? Did the Cro-Magnon people hope that the drawings would bring luck? There is one thing the paintings seem to tell us. The Cro-Magnons had a sense of wonder about the world. They looked at beauty and they understood it.

Main Idea	1		Answer	Score
	Mark the *main idea*		M	15
	Mark the statement that is *too broad*		B	5
	Mark the statement that is *too narrow*		N	5
	a. Cave paintings are beautiful.		☐	_____
	b. The caves of Lascaux hold colorful prehistoric paintings.		☐	_____
	c. Drawings of horses are on the walls of the Lascaux caves.		☐	_____

Score 15 points for each correct answer.   **Score**

Subject Matter   **2**   The main topic of this passage is
- ☐ a. the lives of Cro-Magnon people.
- ☐ b. animals of prehistoric times.
- ☐ c. what the cave paintings of Lascaux looked like.
- ☐ d. the boys who discovered the paintings.   _____

Supporting Details   **3**   Most of the drawings in the caves are of
- ☐ a. several types of animals.
- ☐ b. horses.
- ☐ c. dead people.
- ☐ d. teenage boys.   _____

Conclusion   **4**   The writer would like you to conclude that
- ☐ a. anyone can find cave art.
- ☐ b. the cave paintings of Lascaux are remarkable.
- ☐ c. the Cro-Magnon people are a mystery.
- ☐ d. the Cro-Magnon people were magicians.   _____

Clarifying Devices   **5**   The writer uses the word *you* in the first paragraph to
- ☐ a. give the reader good directions to find the caves.
- ☐ b. pull the reader into the story.
- ☐ c. compare present-day readers with Cro-Magnon people.
- ☐ d. make it clear that this is a true story.   _____

Vocabulary in Context   **6**   The word <u>extraordinary</u> means
- ☐ a. about animals.
- ☐ b. familiar.
- ☐ c. colorful.
- ☐ d. very unusual.   _____

Add your scores for questions 1–6. Enter the total here and on the graph on page 214.   **Total Score**   _____

16 Sea Turtles

Watch where you're walking on the beach. You just might step on a sea turtle nest! Sea turtles are reptiles. They have dry, tough skin and breathe air through lungs. Sea turtles eat or sleep in the ocean. When the female is ready for nesting, she swims to shore. She does this at night, after the hot sun has disappeared. She uses her flippers to drag her heavy body slowly through the sand. When she gets to an area above the high-tide line, she stops. Now she puts her rear flippers to work. She digs a hole one to four feet deep where she lays 50 to 100 eggs. She covers and hides the eggs with sand. Finally, she drags herself back to the ocean, never visiting her nest again.

Back in the nest, the eggs <u>incubate</u> under the warmth of the sun and sand. About two months later, the eggs begin to hatch. The baby turtles are about two inches long and weigh only three-fifths of an ounce. The baby turtles dig their way upward. Under cover of night, they run together toward the reflective brightness of the ocean. Many of the young turtles live in the seaweed in the ocean currents for a few years. Later they move into coastal waters. Only one or two out of about 1,000 young turtles live to adulthood.

There are seven species of sea turtles. The smallest is the ridley. An adult ridley weighs 75 to 100 pounds. The biggest is the leatherback. An adult leatherback weighs about 1,300 pounds and is almost eight feet long.

Sea turtles live in all the oceans except the coldest ones. They nest only in hot tropical and sub-tropical areas. Their powerful, oversized arms let them swim great distances. Some swim hundreds or thousands of miles to feed or nest. Sea turtles don't have teeth. But they have hard, rough jaws that are good for crushing and tearing food. An adult sea turtle lives for 40 to 60 years—much longer than most other animals.

Main Idea	1		
		Answer	**Score**
	Mark the *main idea*	M	15
	Mark the statement that is *too broad*	B	5
	Mark the statement that is *too narrow*	N	5

a. Sea turtles spend much time in the sea but lay their eggs on shore. ☐ _____

b. A female sea turtle lays 50 to 100 eggs. ☐ _____

c. Sea turtles are long-living animals. ☐

Score 15 points for each correct answer.   **Score**

Subject Matter **2** Another good title for this passage would be
- [ ] a. Turtle Watching.
- [ ] b. The Littlest Turtles.
- [ ] c. Sun: A Natural Incubator.
- [ ] d. The Life of a Sea Turtle.   ____

Supporting Details **3** Sea turtles have powerful arms so they can
- [ ] a. lay their eggs.
- [ ] b. fight off sharks and whales.
- [ ] c. swim for thousands of miles.
- [ ] d. float in the ocean currents.   ____

Conclusion **4** What conclusion can you draw from this passage?
- [ ] a. Female sea turtles lay their eggs on shore to hide and protect them.
- [ ] b. Sea turtles are learning to dig deeper nests to protect their eggs.
- [ ] c. Baby sea turtles are afraid to go anywhere without their mothers.
- [ ] d. Sea turtles usually travel in pairs.   ____

Clarifying Devices **5** The author develops ideas in the first paragraph by
- [ ] a. comparing and contrasting.
- [ ] b. using signal and transitional words.
- [ ] c. presenting causes and effects.
- [ ] d. order of importance.   ____

Vocabulary in Context **6** In this passage the word <u>incubate</u> means
- [ ] a. get ready to hatch.
- [ ] b. drown.
- [ ] c. swim.
- [ ] d. come close to dying.   ____

Add your scores for questions 1–6. Enter the total here and on the graph on page 214.   **Total Score** ____

33

17 The Tangram Puzzle

Tangrams are old puzzles. They have been found in Chinese books hundreds of years old. During the 1800s tangrams were very popular in both Europe and the United States. And the puzzles are still enjoyed today.

The tangram puzzle is easy to describe. There are seven different geometric pieces. Five pieces are right triangles. There are two large triangles, one medium triangle, and two small triangles. There are two other pieces, a square and a parallelogram. You move the pieces around to make different shapes. For example, the pieces can make a large square. The tangram square is shown in the diagram at the right.

A book of tangram puzzles shows black outlines of shapes. The challenge is to use all the pieces to make one of the black outlines. There are many geometric shapes to make. Some of the puzzles look like animals and birds. You can also make letters and human figures.

You can buy tangram puzzle pieces made of plastic or wood. But it is easy to make your own set. Draw the pieces on graph paper. Follow the heavy lines in the diagram. Cut the shapes apart. You will have your own set of tangram pieces. As your first puzzle, put the square back together. Next, try making one large triangle. Remember to use all seven pieces. Then try a rectangle.

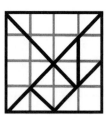

Perhaps you'll find you like working with tangrams. There are many puzzle books using these shapes. Warning: Playing with the pieces can become addictive!

Main Idea	1		
		Answer	Score
Mark the *main idea*		M	15
Mark the statement that is *too broad*		B	5
Mark the statement that is *too narrow*		N	5

a. The seven tangram pieces can make a square. ☐ _____

b. The tangram puzzle is made from seven geometric shapes. ☐ _____

c. People throughout the ages have liked doing puzzles. ☐ _____

Subject Matter   2   This passage is mostly concerned with
- [ ] a. describing how the tangram puzzle works.
- [ ] b. giving hints for solving tangram puzzles.
- [ ] c. the history of puzzles.
- [ ] d. defining figures like squares and triangles.   _____

Supporting Details   3   How many of the tangram pieces are **not** triangles?
- [ ] a. 0
- [ ] b. 1
- [ ] c. 2
- [ ] d. 7   _____

Conclusion   4   From the last paragraph you can conclude that tangram puzzles are
- [ ] a. difficult.
- [ ] b. easy.
- [ ] c. only for children.
- [ ] d. fun for many people.   _____

Clarifying Devices   5   To make a set of tangram puzzle pieces, you need only to
- [ ] a. know the geometric names of the pieces.
- [ ] b. copy the diagram.
- [ ] c. understand geometry.
- [ ] d. use the pieces to make an animal or bird.   _____

Vocabulary in Context   6   In this passage the word <u>parallelogram</u> means
- [ ] a. a three-sided shape.
- [ ] b. a four-sided shape that is not a square.
- [ ] c. a five-sided shape.
- [ ] d. an oval shape.   _____

Add your scores for questions 1–6. Enter the total here and on the graph on page 214.   **Total Score**   _____

18 The Work of an Architect

Think about the place you live. It may be a small house or a large apartment. You may find it ugly or beautiful. Now think of a building that has caught your eye. Something about that building's appearance must have impressed you. Houses, apartment buildings, and shopping malls all have one thing in common. An architect probably decided how they would look and be built.

What do architects do? They don't actually build buildings. (Contractors are responsible for that.) But they do design them. They draw the plans to show the size of floors and the height of rooms. They decide where doors and windows will go. They choose the materials for the outside walls and the roof. They may create a scale model of the building so the client can see what it will look like. Or they may draw a model on a computer. Small, simple buildings are not always designed by architects. But larger, more <u>complex</u> ones nearly always are.

When did people first start using architects? Clearly, early people put together their own houses. They used whatever materials they had. Some houses were square. They were made of wood and covered with skins. Some were round and made of stone. But all had small rooms, low ceilings, and few windows. No one knew how to build a structure with large openings. They didn't know how to support high, wide ceilings.

The earliest architect we know about lived in ancient Egypt. His name was Imhotep. He lived about 2700 B.C. He designed the first pyramid and many other burial structures. Buildings today, of course, look very different. But architects have kept on learning and trying new designs.

Main Idea	1		Answer	Score
	Mark the *main idea*		M	15
	Mark the statement that is *too broad*		B	5
	Mark the statement that is *too narrow*		N	5
	a. Architecture has a long history.		☐	_____
	b. The earliest architect we know about was Imhotep.		☐	_____
	c. From early times, the job of an architect has been to plan and design buildings.		☐	_____

Score 15 points for each correct answer.   **Score**

Subject Matter 2 This passage is mostly about
- ☐ a. the work of Imhotep.
- ☐ b. why early buildings were simple structures.
- ☐ c. what architects do.
- ☐ d. the difference between architects and contractors.   _____

Supporting Details 3 Imhotep lived
- ☐ a. in the early 20th century.
- ☐ b. in the Middle Ages.
- ☐ c. about 1700 A.D.
- ☐ d. about 2700 B.C.   _____

Conclusion 4 Which of these buildings would an architect most likely have designed?
- ☐ a. a gas station
- ☐ b. a skyscraper
- ☐ c. a garage
- ☐ d. a ticket office   _____

Clarifying Devices 5 The word *But* in the last sentence of the second paragraph signals that the sentence will present
- ☐ a. more information on the same topic.
- ☐ b. contrasting information.
- ☐ c. a choice.
- ☐ d. a surprising fact.   _____

Vocabulary in Context 6 In this passage <u>complex</u> means
- ☐ a. complicated.
- ☐ b. a large group of buildings.
- ☐ c. simple.
- ☐ d. beautiful.   _____

Add your scores for questions 1–6. Enter the total here and on the graph on page 214.   **Total Score** _____

19 A Separation of Powers

The United States Constitution was written in 1787. The writer, James Madison, wanted a strong government. It would have three branches. One would be the president. A second would be the courts. A third would make laws. This third branch would represent the people.

How many representatives would there be? Madison said the number should reflect how many people live in a state. New Jersey had few people. These people did not agree. They said each state should have the same number of representatives. The people of Connecticut wanted a compromise. They said the law-making branch should have two parts. In one part, each state would have the same number of members. In the other part, the number of members from a state would vary. Large states would have more members. Small states would have fewer. The states agreed.

The three branches balance each other's power. No branch has all the power. The states <u>adopted</u> this plan in 1789. Here is what each branch does.

The *executive branch* is the office of the President. (It also includes his or her cabinet.) This branch enforces federal laws. It appoints federal officials. It deals with foreign countries. The President is commander of the armed forces.

The *judicial branch* includes the Supreme Court. It also includes the lower Federal Courts. It decides cases of law.

The *legislative branch* makes laws. It also amends and repeals laws and collects taxes. One part of this branch is the Senate. It has 100 members. Each state has two senators. The other part is the House of Representatives. It has 435 members. Each state sends a number of representatives based on its population.

Main Idea	1		Answer	Score
	Mark the *main idea*		M	15
	Mark the statement that is *too broad*		B	5
	Mark the statement that is *too narrow*		N	5

a. The U.S. Constitution provides for three branches of government. ☐ _____

b. The United States has a Constitution. ☐ _____

c. The Senate has 100 members. ☐ _____

Subject Matter   2   Another good title for this passage is
- ☐ a. A Battle Among the States.
- ☐ b. James Madison, American Hero.
- ☐ c. Three Branches Equals One Government.
- ☐ d. More than 200 Years Ago.   _____

Supporting Details   3   The legislative branch deals mainly with
- ☐ a. the armed forces.
- ☐ b. the making of laws.
- ☐ c. the courts.
- ☐ d. foreign policy.   _____

Conclusion   4   Which statement best describes the final Constitution?
- ☐ a. It uses only James Madison's ideas.
- ☐ b. It is a compromise among the states.
- ☐ c. It does not represent small states.
- ☐ d. It gives most of the power to the President.   _____

Clarifying Devices   5   In this passage, the words *legislative branch* are in italic type as an example of
- ☐ a. a main title.
- ☐ b. a quotation.
- ☐ c. an author's byline.
- ☐ d. an important term.   _____

Vocabulary in Context   6   The word <u>adopted</u> in this passage means
- ☐ a. formally and officially approved.
- ☐ b. raised another's child as one's own.
- ☐ c. chosen for use in a classroom.
- ☐ d. admired greatly.   _____

Add your scores for questions 1–6. Enter the total here and on the graph on page 214.   **Total Score**   _____

20 Fossils

Scientists know much about the earth's history. They estimate that plants and animals lived as long as 3.5 billion years ago. Relatives of some modern animals lived 580 million years ago. Dinosaurs lived about 200 million years ago. The first humans came along about 3.7 million years ago. How do scientists know all this? They find clues in the earth's rocks. Rocks often contain fossils, the preserved remains of things that lived long ago.

Most fossils are the hard parts of living things. Animal bones, teeth, and shells may be fossils. Fossils of plant parts are rare. Plants don't have hard parts. But plant imprints and animal tracks in hardened mud are fossils. Sometimes fossils are whole animals. For example, whole woolly mammoths have been found. They became trapped when glaciers of ice moved across the earth.

Most fossils are found in sedimentary rock. Why? Dead plants and animals fell into lakes and oceans. Sediment, such as sand or mud, covered them. Over time, many layers of sediments collected. The upper layers pushed down on the lower layers. The sediment in the lower layers changed into rock. Bones, teeth, and shells became fossils in the rock. Sometimes a dead animal's body decayed. The body left its shape in the rock. This space is a type of fossil called a mold. Sediments may seep into a mold and harden. This type of fossil is called a cast.

Fossils of ocean animals have been found on mountains. How did they get there? The earth's <u>crust</u> is always moving. The sedimentary rock in lakes and oceans moves with it. That's why fossils of ocean plants and animals can be found on land.

Main Idea	1		
		Answer	**Score**
	Mark the *main idea*	M	15
	Mark the statement that is *too broad*	B	5
	Mark the statement that is *too narrow*	N	5

a. Fossils are clues to what long-ago animals and plants looked like. ☐ _____

b. Scientists know much about the earth's history. ☐ _____

c. Fossils of whole woolly mammoths have been found. ☐ _____

Subject Matter   **2**   This passage is mostly concerned with
- ☐ a. woolly mammoths.
- ☐ b. sedimentary rock.
- ☐ c. fossils.
- ☐ d. ocean animals.   _____

Supporting Details   **3**   Which of the following is **not** a type of fossil?
- ☐ a. a plant imprint
- ☐ b. a mold
- ☐ c. an animal's shell
- ☐ d. a sediment   _____

Conclusion   **4**   We can conclude from this passage that scientists have
- ☐ a. made fossils out of sand and mud.
- ☐ b. studied fossils of ancient plants and animals.
- ☐ c. melted glaciers of ice.
- ☐ d. created dinosaurs in the laboratory.   _____

Clarifying Devices   **5**   The author begins this passage by giving
- ☐ a. facts about life long ago.
- ☐ b. examples of fossils.
- ☐ c. descriptions of glaciers.
- ☐ d. a step-by-step explanation.   _____

Vocabulary in Context   **6**   In this passage the word <u>crust</u> means
- ☐ a. water.
- ☐ b. part of a piece of bread.
- ☐ c. having a lot of nerve.
- ☐ d. hard outer layer.   _____

Add your scores for questions 1–6. Enter the total here and on the graph on page 214.   **Total Score**   _____

21 Calculators and Repeating Decimals

Calculators are great tools. They help you do math quickly. They show exact answers to difficult problems. Are calculators always right? It depends on what you mean by right. You may be adding, subtracting, or multiplying. Then a calculator will show the exact answer. But dividing is different. Try dividing 10 by 6 on a calculator. You may get 1.6666666. Or you may get 1.6666667. Which is the exact answer, 1.6666666 or 1.6666667? Neither! Both are approximations. They are both right. But neither is exact.

Why do calculators do this? Most of them can't show fractions. The exact answer to 10 divided by 6 is the mixed number $1^2/_3$. The calculator has no way to <u>display</u> two-thirds.

$$6\overline{)10.00\ldots}^{\,1.66\ldots}$$
$$\underline{-6}$$
$$40$$
$$\underline{-36}$$
$$40$$
$$\underline{-36}$$
$$4\ldots$$

Here is a way to understand what is happening. Divide 10 by 6 using paper and pencil. Your problem will look like the one at the left. The answer has a repeating decimal. You can keep dividing forever. You'll never get an exact answer. The digit 6 in the answer repeats forever.

A calculator that gives 1.6666666 is truncating (cutting off) the answer. It shows as many digits as it can. Then it drops the rest. A calculator that gives 1.6666667 is rounding. Since the last digit is 5 or greater, it shows the next higher digit (7).

For most division problems, it won't matter if the answer is approximate. But you might have a problem in which you really need the exact answer. Then you may need to use fractions.

Main Idea   1

	Answer	Score
Mark the *main idea*	M	15
Mark the statement that is *too broad*	B	5
Mark the statement that is *too narrow*	N	5

a. Dividing 10 by 6 results in a repeating decimal. ☐ _____

b. Calculators are useful tools in math. ☐ _____

c. In division problems, calculators sometimes give approximate answers. ☐ _____

42

Subject Matter   **2**   This passage is mainly about
- [ ] a. how to round off answers.
- [ ] b. multiplying with fractions.
- [ ] c. dividing numbers on a calculator.
- [ ] d. checking answers with a calculator.

_____

Supporting Details   **3**   A calculator answer of 1.6666667 is probably
- [ ] a. rounded.
- [ ] b. truncated.
- [ ] c. exact.
- [ ] d. not correct.

_____

Conclusion   **4**   What can you conclude from this passage?
- [ ] a. You should never divide numbers with a calculator.
- [ ] b. When you divide with a calculator, the answer may be approximate.
- [ ] c. All division problems have repeating decimals as answers.
- [ ] d. Exact answers are not important in division.

_____

Clarifying Devices   **5**   In the first paragraph the writer shows the difference in meaning between right and
- [ ] a. wrong.
- [ ] b. exact.
- [ ] c. division.
- [ ] d. calculate.

_____

Vocabulary in Context   **6**   In this passage the word <u>display</u> means
- [ ] a. draw a picture of.
- [ ] b. put into a store window.
- [ ] c. correct.
- [ ] d. show.

_____

Add your scores for questions 1–6. Enter the total here and on the graph on page 214.   **Total Score**

_____

22 Capital of the Inca Empire

Cuzco was the capital city of the Inca Empire in South America. The empire began in the 1300s. It ended suddenly in 1532. At its peak the empire had 12 million people. Peru, Ecuador, and parts of Chile, Bolivia, and Argentina made up the empire. The city of Cuzco was the <u>hub</u>. Inca roads spread from the city like spokes on a wheel. The roads went to the four corners of the empire. The roads brought the empire's treasure of silver and gold into Cuzco.

Cuzco had palaces, temples, and government buildings. The most important buildings were made from fine stonework. Inca architects planned these buildings. First they made clay models. Then workers dug huge blocks of limestone and granite from the ground. Next skilled stonemasons cut and fit the blocks together. The stonemasons shaped each stone. They used stone hammers and bronze chisels. Thousands of workers hauled the blocks into place. Stone blocks weighed as much as 20 tons. The workers moved the blocks with ropes and wooden rollers. To get heavy stones to the top of high walls, workers dragged them up earth ramps. Incas sanded and polished the stone blocks. The blocks fit together perfectly. There were no gaps or spaces. Only a line showed where the blocks were joined.

The Spaniards destroyed much of Cuzco in 1533. They built a new, Spanish city on top of the old one. Some of their buildings have the old Inca buildings as their foundations. Sometimes they used the Incas' stones to build new buildings. They used Inca gold and silver to decorate their churches. The empire is gone now, but Incan skill and wealth remain.

Main Idea   1

	Answer	Score
Mark the *main idea*	M	15
Mark the statement that is *too broad*	B	5
Mark the statement that is *too narrow*	N	5

a. Cuzco was a city in the Inca Empire. ☐ _____

b. The Spaniards decorated their churches with Inca gold. ☐ _____

c. The buildings of Cuzco were built with skill and wealth. ☐ _____

Subject Matter   **2**   This passage is mainly about
- ☐ a. the Spanish destruction of Cuzco.
- ☐ b. the skill of Inca builders.
- ☐ c. the location of the Inca Empire.
- ☐ d. the modern city of Cuzco.   _____

Supporting Details   **3**   Buildings in the Inca city of Cuzco were
- ☐ a. made of clay.
- ☐ b. homes for 12 million people.
- ☐ c. made of fine stonework.
- ☐ d. built quickly.   _____

Conclusion   **4**   In the last paragraph, the phrase "Incan skill and wealth remain" means
- ☐ a. Incas still live and work in Cuzco.
- ☐ b. Spaniards love the Incan treasures.
- ☐ c. buildings and gold are preserved in museums.
- ☐ d. Inca stone blocks and gold still exist in Cuzco.   _____

Clarifying Devices   **5**   The Incan roads are compared to
- ☐ a. the spokes of a wheel.
- ☐ b. stone hammers and bronze chisels.
- ☐ c. four corners of an empire.
- ☐ d. the treasures of gold and silver.   _____

Vocabulary in Context   **6**   In this passage the word <u>hub</u> means the
- ☐ a. best.
- ☐ b. center of importance.
- ☐ c. noisy part of the empire.
- ☐ d. center of a wheel.   _____

Add your scores for questions 1–6. Enter the total here and on the graph on page 214.   Total Score   _____

23 Lightning

A flash of bright light zigzags from a cloud. A crash of thunder echoes seconds later. Lightning and thunder make most people jumpy. In early America, Benjamin Franklin linked lightning to science. During a thunderstorm, he flew a kite. He tied a key to the end of the string. Franklin saw sparks jump from the key. He thought the sky was electrically charged. The electric charges went down the string to the key. His work was crucial to understanding lightning. He learned that lightning is an electrical current.

Today we know more. Lightning forms in clouds. A cloud has charged energy in it. The energy at the top of a cloud is positive. The energy at the bottom is negative. Opposites attract. So the positive and negative charges move toward each other. When they meet, they make an electric current. The current forms a bolt of lightning. The bolt moves from the bottom of the cloud. It has a negative charge. We can't see the bolt, but it reaches downward. Positive energy from the ground moves up. When the opposite charges meet, a powerful electric current flows between them. That causes a flash of lightning. Its temperature is about 50,000 degrees Fahrenheit. That's almost five times hotter than the surface of the sun! The lightning heats the air around it. The heated air quickly expands. As it moves, it causes a shock wave. That's the thunder we hear.

Lightning kills about 200 people in the United States each year. It injures about 700 people. These tips can help you be safe. When lightning strikes, don't stand under a tree. Stay away from metal objects. Get out of and away from pools and lakes. Move into a building or get inside a car. Indoors, stay away from windows and doors. Unplug electrical appliances. Stay off the telephone. Seek immediate medical attention for anyone struck by lightning. Remember, lightning kills. So play it safe!

Main Idea   1

	Answer	Score
Mark the *main idea*	M	15
Mark the statement that is *too broad*	B	5
Mark the statement that is *too narrow*	N	5

a. Lightning kills about 200 people in the United States each year. ☐ _____

b. Lightning and thunder are weather events. ☐ _____

c. Lightning is a dangerous electric current between clouds and the earth. ☐ _____

Score 15 points for each correct answer.   **Score**

Subject Matter 2 This passage is mainly about
☐ a. similarities between thunder and lightning.
☐ b. why Ben Franklin flew a kite in a storm.
☐ c. what lightning is and how to be safe from it.
☐ d. why the temperature of lightning is greater than the temperature of the sun.

_____

Supporting Details 3 A lightning bolt results when
☐ a. the temperature reaches 50,000 degrees Fahrenheit.
☐ b. negative and positive energy come together.
☐ c. a key is attached to a kite.
☐ d. people stand under a tree during a storm.

_____

Conclusion 4 The sentence "Opposites attract." suggests that negatively charged energy
☐ a. is attracted to thunder.
☐ b. forms a lightning bolt.
☐ c. quickly heats the air around it.
☐ d. will move toward positively charged energy.

_____

Clarifying Devices 5 The first two sentences of this passage
☐ a. are exaggerations.
☐ b. help you imagine a thunderstorm.
☐ c. take you back into United States history.
☐ d. explain the meaning of the word _jumpy_.

_____

Vocabulary in Context 6 The word crucial means
☐ a. extremely wet.
☐ b. not meaningful.
☐ c. very important.
☐ d. dark and stormy.

_____

Add your scores for questions 1–6. Enter the total here and on the graph on page 214.   **Total Score**

_____

24 The Earliest Theater

Plays are not a new thing. People have been putting them on for thousands of years. Plays first came on the scene in the sixth century B.C. They were put on in Greece.

How did the first plays develop? They were part of festivals to honor the gods. There were games, dancing, and songs sung by a chorus. Then someone got an idea. Instead of just the chorus singing, people could also speak lines to each other. This was the beginning of dialogue. And dialogue is a basic ingredient of drama.

So the early Greek plays had regular characters and a chorus. The story happened through the main characters. But the chorus commented on or explained the action. For instance, one character might treat another cruelly. The chorus might admonish the character that the gods did not approve of such behavior.

The stories in the plays were mostly about the gods or famous heroes. These were stories the audience already knew. Many of the characters in these stories were women. But there were no women actors. Both the main characters and the chorus were played by men.

Greek theaters were usually built into hillsides. The stage was at the bottom. The seats rose up the side of the hill. These theaters were often very large. It could be hard to see and hear. Actors wore platform shoes. These made them look taller. They also wore tall headdresses and masks. A mask would be painted with a face showing the character's feelings. It would also have a mouth opening shaped like a funnel. This made the actor's voice sound louder. There was a small painted building on the stage. Actors could go in and out one of its three doors. Aside from this, there was no scenery.

Main Idea	1		Answer	Score
	Mark the *main idea*		M	15
	Mark the statement that is *too broad*		B	5
	Mark the statement that is *too narrow*		N	5

a. Early Greek theaters were built into the sides of hills. ☐ _____

b. The earliest plays were put on thousands of years ago. ☐ _____

c. Early Greek theater developed ways of presenting characters, costumes, and staging. ☐ _____

Score 15 points for each correct answer.   **Score**

Subject Matter   **2**   Another good title for this passage would be
- ☐ a. Plays Then and Now.
- ☐ b. Performing in a Large Theater.
- ☐ c. Early Greek Theater.
- ☐ d. The Actors' Use of Masks.   _____

Supporting Details   **3**   The first part of a play to be developed was
- ☐ a. the chorus.
- ☐ b. dialogue.
- ☐ c. masks.
- ☐ d. scenery.   _____

Conclusion   **4**   Actors wore platform shoes and masks to
- ☐ a. show how important the characters were.
- ☐ b. make it easier for audiences to see them.
- ☐ c. make them stand out from the chorus.
- ☐ d. make it easier for audiences to laugh at them.   _____

Clarifying Devices   **5**   In the third paragraph, the characters and the chorus are explained by
- ☐ a. describing how they dressed.
- ☐ b. describing their functions.
- ☐ c. telling in what ways they were similar.
- ☐ d. telling why women could not participate.   _____

Vocabulary in Context   **6**   <u>Admonish</u> means
- ☐ a. warn.
- ☐ b. tease.
- ☐ c. lie to.
- ☐ d. notice.   _____

Add your scores for questions 1–6. Enter the total here and on the graph on page 214.   **Total Score**   _____

49

25 Will Roman Numerals Return?

You've probably seen Roman numerals. But you haven't seen them very often. You can buy clocks and watches with Roman numerals. They use Roman numerals I (1) through XII (12) for the hours. The front pages in a book sometimes have Roman numerals for page numbers. Roman numerals can be also found on buildings. There they show the date the building was made. And some older movies and books use them. They show the copyright date.

The Roman system was developed by the ancient Romans. It uses the letters I, V, X, L, C, D, and M to stand for 1, 5, 10, 50, 100, 500, and 1000. Other numbers are made by combining the letters in different ways. The number 8 is VIII, formed by adding three ones to V. Sometimes subtraction is used. The numbers 4 and 9 are made this way. Four is five minus one, or IV. Nine is ten minus one, or IX. Notice that the part being subtracted comes first.

Roman numerals for dates can be very long. The year 1938 is written MCMXXXVIII. Dates in the 1800s are even worse. The date 1888 is written MDCCCLXXXVIII. Is isn't difficult to see why people stopped using Roman numerals for dates.

But numbers go in and out of <u>fashion</u>. Now that the 1900s have come to an end, Roman numerals may again have their turn. The year 2000 is a simple MM. The next ten years are pretty easy too. Here is how the list begins. First is MMI, then MMII, MMIII, MMIV, MMV.

The year 2000 was nicknamed Y2K. (K stands for 1000.) But 2000 could just as easily have been called MM. This is a shorter—and more tasty-sounding—abbreviation.

Main Idea	1	Answer	Score
	Mark the *main idea*	M	15
	Mark the statement that is *too broad*	B	5
	Mark the statement that is *too narrow*	N	5
	a. Roman numerals may be used more frequently in the future.	☐	_____
	b. Roman numerals use letters to stand for numbers.	☐	_____
	c. Dates can be written in many different ways.	☐	_____

Score 15 points for each correct answer. **Score**

Subject Matter **2** This passage is mostly concerned with
- [ ] a. the meaning of Y2K.
- [ ] b. telling time using Roman numerals.
- [ ] c. how Roman numerals are written and used.
- [ ] d. adding and subtracting Roman numerals. _____

Supporting Details **3** The Roman numeral D stands for
- [ ] a. 10.
- [ ] b. 50.
- [ ] c. 500.
- [ ] d. 5000. _____

Conclusion **4** The Roman numeral VL equals
- [ ] a. 15 (5 is added to 10).
- [ ] b. 55 (5 is added to 50).
- [ ] c. 45 (5 is subtracted from 50).
- [ ] d. 95 (5 is subtracted from 100). _____

Clarifying Devices **5** The writer explains how Roman numerals are made by
- [ ] a. showing diagrams.
- [ ] b. relating them to clocks and watches.
- [ ] c. proving mathematical statements.
- [ ] d. giving examples. _____

Vocabulary in Context **6** In this passage the word <u>fashion</u> means
- [ ] a. relating to clothing.
- [ ] b. to create or make.
- [ ] c. style or trend.
- [ ] d. not in current use. _____

Add your scores for questions 1–6. Enter the total here **Total**
and on the graph on page 214. **Score** _____

26 What Is Social Studies?

A 1987 <u>survey</u> was given to 5,000 high school seniors. It showed that they did not know geography. Students in Boston were questioned. One-third of them could not name six New England states. Students in Baltimore were questioned. Half could not shade in the United States on a map. Here is what another survey showed. Students did not know history. Most did not know the dates of the American Civil War. Many did not know World War II leaders.

Someone else asked this question. What did students think of social studies? Their answer: Social studies was not important. They said it was the least important of their studies.

What is social studies? It is the study of individuals. It is the study of groups. It is the study of societies. Social studies covers many fields. You have read about history and geography. These are part of social studies. It covers many other areas as well. Let's say you study the way people live together in groups. This is an area of social studies. So is learning about very early people. So is studying government.

Is social studies important? Early Americans thought so. Students then learned history and civics. This was to make them good citizens. A report from 1916 set a new goal. It said, "The social studies should cultivate a sense of membership in the world community." The world community is very large. But today it is easy to share ideas in it. We have radio and TV. We have phones. We have computers.

Social studies helps us understand the world's people. It helps us know groups and societies. The 1916 goal was important then. It is even more important now. We all need to be good world citizens.

Main Idea	1	Answer	Score
	Mark the *main idea*	M	15
	Mark the statement that is *too broad*	B	5
	Mark the statement that is *too narrow*	N	5

a. Social studies includes many areas of study about people and how they live. ☐ _____

b. A report from 1916 set a new goal for learning social studies. ☐ _____

c. Social studies is an important field. ☐ _____

Score 15 points for each correct answer.   Score

Subject Matter   **2**   Social studies
☐ a. uses radios, TVs, and computers.
☐ b. is the study of people, groups, and societies.
☐ c. can be understood by questioning students.
☐ d. was first taught in 1916.   _____

Supporting   **3**   Which fact supports the statement that students
Details   did not know geography?
☐ a. A survey questioned 5,000 students.
☐ b. Most students did not know when the
          Civil War was.
☐ c. Many students did not know World
          War II leaders.
☐ d. Half of the students from Baltimore could
          not locate the United States on a map.   _____

Conclusion   **4**   This passage makes it clear that
☐ a. we are not members of a world community.
☐ b. social studies helps make good world citizens.
☐ c. researchers should question more students.
☐ d. social studies is not important.   _____

Clarifying   **5**   The quotation marks around the sentence "The
Devices   social studies should cultivate a sense of membership
                         in the world community." show that it
☐ a. is important.
☐ b. is the writer's opinion.
☐ c. is the exact words from the 1916 report.
☐ d. was spoken by a high school student.   _____

Vocabulary   **6**   The word <u>survey</u> in this passage means a
in Context
☐ a. general look.
☐ b. plan showing size, shape, and boundaries.
☐ c. formal study or poll.
☐ d. discussion.   _____

Add your scores for questions 1–6. Enter the total here   **Total**
and on the graph on page 215.   **Score**   _____

53

27 Identifying the *Danaus plexippus*

This creature is found anywhere in the world where it's not too hot or too cold. It has six legs and four orange-and-black wings. Its color suggested its name: King William of Holland was the Prince of Orange—the future monarch of England. The creature is a daytime traveler but only in good conditions. It takes shelter during rainstorms. When it flies, it flutters. It glides and soars through the air. Airplane pilots have spotted it as high as three-quarters of a mile above the earth. Its speed of 12 miles per hour isn't as fast as a bird. It's impressive, though, since this creature weighs only seven ounces. It goes the distance too. It may cover 80 miles in one day. Long trips of 1,500 miles are common in late summer. For energy, it sips nectar from flowers. At the same time it carries pollen from plant to plant. This helps the plants produce more seeds, which become plants. Have you figured out what this amazing insect is? Its scientific name is *Danaus plexippus,* but it's better known as the monarch butterfly.

Monarchs can live up to nine months, though most live only two to five weeks. Females are very busy during that time. They lay about 700 eggs, one egg at a time. Each egg is laid on a different milkweed plant. When the egg hatches, a caterpillar comes out. It is an "eating machine." It eats its shell. It eats the milkweed plant on which it was laid. Eating is about all it does until it is fully grown. Then it attaches itself to a twig. The caterpillar forms a <u>chrysalis</u> around itself. Like a moth's cocoon, a chrysalis protects the caterpillar. Inside the chrysalis, the caterpillar changes into a butterfly. Next the butterfly splits open the chrysalis and crawls out. It hangs onto the chrysalis for about two hours until its wings dry. The change from egg to caterpillar to chrysalis to butterfly takes three to four weeks. Finally the monarch is ready to fly.

Main Idea   1

	Answer	Score
Mark the *main idea*	M	15
Mark the statement that is *too broad*	B	5
Mark the statement that is *too narrow*	N	5

a. The monarch butterfly was named after King William, the Prince of Orange. ☐ _____

b. The high-flying monarch goes through several changes from egg to butterfly. ☐ _____

c. Monarchs are a type of butterfly. ☐ _____

Score 15 points for each correct answer.   **Score**

Subject Matter   2   Another good title for this passage would be
- [ ] a. Butterflies.
- [ ] b. A Nectar Drinker.
- [ ] c. Cocoon.
- [ ] d. The Remarkable Monarch.   _____

Supporting Details   3   Which of the following shows the order in which a butterfly develops?
- [ ] a. butterfly to egg to caterpillar to chrysalis
- [ ] b. butterfly to egg to chrysalis to caterpillar
- [ ] c. egg to caterpillar to chrysalis to butterfly
- [ ] d. egg to chrysalis to caterpillar to butterfly   _____

Conclusion   4   We can conclude from this passage that monarchs
- [ ] a. eat a lot of plants but also help plants to reproduce.
- [ ] b. are the world's largest butterflies.
- [ ] c. need a scientific name that is more descriptive.
- [ ] d. have trouble flying at high altitudes.   _____

Clarifying Devices   5   The author explains the phrase "eating machine" by presenting
- [ ] a. a strong argument.
- [ ] b. examples.
- [ ] c. precise measurements.
- [ ] d. a scientific study.   _____

Vocabulary in Context   6   A chrysalis is a
- [ ] a. crystal.
- [ ] b. stem for caterpillars to crawl on.
- [ ] c. protective shelter for a caterpillar.
- [ ] d. monarch butterfly.   _____

Add your scores for questions 1–6. Enter the total here and on the graph on page 215.   **Total Score**   _____

28 What Michelangelo Did

You probably know what a sculpture is. It is a figure made by carving or modeling. Do you know who was the greatest sculptor of all time? Nearly everyone agrees. It was Michelangelo. He was an Italian who lived from 1475 to 1564.

Michelangelo began his artistic training early. He began to study painting when he was 13. After a year, his training as a sculptor began. It included studying corpses to learn about the human body. Sculptors of that time carved in stone, usually marble. So did Michelangelo. By age 16 he had already produced two works.

One of his most famous sculptures is the Pietà. This is in St. Peter's Church in Rome. It is a statue of the Virgin Mary holding the dead Christ. His body rests across her lap. The detail on the statue is amazing. The two figures look very lifelike. Their arms and legs look natural, not posed. Mary has a sad expression on her face. But she seems <u>restrained</u>. She will be able to bear her grief. Michelangelo carved this masterpiece before he was 25 years old.

Another of his great works is the statue of David. (David is the young boy in the Bible who killed the giant Goliath.) This huge sculpture is more than 14 feet tall. It was made for the city of Florence. It was to be a symbol. Times were hard in the city. Its citizens had to be alert to danger. In the sculpture, David looks ready for battle. He is ready to throw the stone that killed Goliath. This statue is the pride of Florence. It took three years to carve.

Though primarily a sculptor, Michelangelo also did some remarkable painting. On the ceiling of the Sistine Chapel in Rome, he painted stories from the Bible. This work included over 300 figures. And he painted it lying flat on his back on a scaffold!

Main Idea	1	Answer	Score
	Mark the *main idea*	M	15
	Mark the statement that is *too broad*	B	5
	Mark the statement that is *too narrow*	N	5
	a. Michelangelo was a sculptor.	☐	_____
	b. Michelangelo sculpted two of the world's most famous statues.	☐	_____
	c. Michelangelo's statue of David was carved for the city of Florence.	☐	_____

Score 15 points for each correct answer.   Score

Subject Matter   **2**   This passage is mostly about
- ☐ a. Michelangelo's works and his early training.
- ☐ b. life in 16th century Italy.
- ☐ c. the Pietà.
- ☐ d. Michelangelo's talents as a painter.   _____

Supporting Details   **3**   The statue of David
- ☐ a. shows David battling Goliath.
- ☐ b. no longer exists.
- ☐ c. was carved before Michelangelo was 25.
- ☐ d. is more than 14 feet tall.   _____

Conclusion   **4**   You can conclude from this passage that during Michelangelo's time,
- ☐ a. students could learn a trade when they were young.
- ☐ b. few people appreciated sculpture.
- ☐ c. sculpture was more important than painting.
- ☐ d. there were a lot of wars.   _____

Clarifying Devices   **5**   The author helps you appreciate two of Michelangelo's statues by
- ☐ a. telling what they are made of.
- ☐ b. describing what they look like.
- ☐ c. explaining how sculpture is done.
- ☐ d. telling why Michelangelo carved each of them.   _____

Vocabulary in Context   **6**   In this passage restrained means
- ☐ a. held down with ropes.
- ☐ b. beautifully carved.
- ☐ c. in control of oneself.
- ☐ d. shipped by train.   _____

Add your scores for questions 1–6. Enter the total here and on the graph on page 215.   Total Score   _____

29 The Digits of Pi

You may have a calculator with a pi key. This key shows the symbol π, which is a letter from the Greek alphabet. Why is π on one of the calculator keys?

Pi is a number that shows how parts of a circle relate to each other. To understand pi, imagine a circle. Now imagine a line through the middle that cuts the circle in half. This line is the diameter. To find a value for pi, use a soup can. The top or bottom of the can is a circle. Put a string around the circular part and measure it. This gives the circumference of the circle, or the distance around it. Now measure the diameter of the can. Divide the circumference by the diameter and you'll have a value for pi.

The value of pi is a constant. It never changes. It doesn't matter how big a circle is. When you divide the circumference by the diameter, you'll get pi. But what number does pi equal? For any circle, dividing the circumference by the diameter will give the appropriate value of pi as 3.14 or $\frac{22}{7}$.

For thousands of years people have worked on finding more and more <u>precise</u> values for pi. You may have used 3.14 as the value in a math class. A more precise value is 3.1415926535897931. In 1844 a German man spent two months finding the first 200 digits of pi. In 1947, D. F. Ferguson raised the number of digits to 808.

Today, using computers, people have found hundreds of millions of digits. Since pi is an irrational number, the digits will never repeat in a pattern. So people who are fascinated can keep working on pi. There will never be a last digit for it.

Main Idea	1	Answer	Score
	Mark the *main idea*	M	15
	Mark the statement that is *too broad*	B	5
	Mark the statement that is *too narrow*	N	5

a. The value of pi is a constant that we can figure out more and more exactly. ☐ _____

b. One value of pi is 3.1415926535897931. ☐ _____

c. Pi is a constant number. ☐ _____

Score 15 points for each correct answer.   **Score**

Subject Matter   **2**   This passage is mostly concerned with
- ☐ a. different parts of circles.
- ☐ b. figuring out the value of pi.
- ☐ c. dividing numbers.
- ☐ d. patterns in numbers.   _____

Supporting Details   **3**   The circumference of a circle is
- ☐ a. the distance across the center.
- ☐ b. less than the diameter.
- ☐ c. always less than 4 units.
- ☐ d. the distance around the outside.   _____

Conclusion   **4**   Based on information in the passage, you can conclude that the value of pi
- ☐ a. is closer to 3 than to 4.
- ☐ b. is closer to 4 than to 3.
- ☐ c. is exactly equal to 3.14.
- ☐ d. has different values in different situations.   _____

Clarifying Devices   **5**   The writer shows that pi must be less than 4 by
- ☐ a. describing the history of calculations for pi.
- ☐ b. explaining what diameter means.
- ☐ c. using an example.
- ☐ d. explaining that π is a Greek letter.   _____

Vocabulary in Context   **6**   In this passage the word <u>precise</u> means
- ☐ a. difficult.
- ☐ b. exact.
- ☐ c. having a pattern.
- ☐ d. lengthy.   _____

Add your scores for questions 1–6. Enter the total here and on the graph on page 215.   **Total Score**   _____

30 The Fertile Crescent

Eleven thousand years ago, the area called the Fertile Crescent may have seemed an unlikely place to live and farm. This flat land in the Middle East was barren and dry. The clay soil was hard. Rain was scarce. So why did one of the first civilizations begin here?

Much of the Fertile Crescent is between two rivers. These are the Tigris and the Euphrates. How could people get the river water to their dry fields? They needed canals, ditches, or pipes to carry water to the dry land. This is called irrigation. With irrigation, people could grow crops.

Irrigation caused farming in the Fertile Crescent to become more successful. Farmers grew many crops. They grew barley, wheat, vegetables, date palms, and grapevines. There was plenty of food. As a result, several things happened.

One result was this: People were no longer hungry. They could store food for times when the crops did not do well.

Another result was that people could have other skills. Not everyone had to be a farmer. People could be gem cutters, metal workers, or carpenters. They could be judges, doctors, or musicians.

And so the population increased. Cities grew. Leaders organized the people. Canals were planned, built, and taken care of. The people needed leaders to get these jobs done.

As time went on, people could trade <u>surplus</u> grain for things they did not grow or make. They could trade for timber, stone, gems, and metals.

All these things made a civilization. That is why this area, the Fertile Crescent, is where one of the world's first civilizations began.

Main Idea	1			Answer	Score
		Mark the *main idea*		M	15
		Mark the statement that is *too broad*		B	5
		Mark the statement that is *too narrow*		N	5

a. Successful farming led to one of the world's first civilizations.	☐	___
b. The Fertile Crescent is between the Tigris and Euphrates rivers.	☐	___
c. Civilization depends on farming.	☐	___

Subject Matter 2 This passage is mainly about
- ☐ a. irrigation.
- ☐ b. the beginnings of trade.
- ☐ c. why a civilization like the Fertile Crescent developed.
- ☐ d. the growth of a city.

_____

Supporting Details 3 Farming was successful because
- ☐ a. cities grew.
- ☐ b. the people could learn new trades.
- ☐ c. the people had leaders.
- ☐ d. irrigation brought water to dry land.

_____

Conclusion 4 This passage suggests that
- ☐ a. civilizations can develop anywhere.
- ☐ b. big cities are better than small cities.
- ☐ c. as civilizations grow, they no longer need farms.
- ☐ d. certain conditions are necessary for a civilization.

_____

Clarifying Devices 5 The writer introduces the topic of the passage by
- ☐ a. asking a question in the first paragraph.
- ☐ b. asking a question in the second paragraph.
- ☐ c. defining irrigation.
- ☐ d. listing several results.

_____

Vocabulary in Context 6 The word <u>surplus</u> means
- ☐ a. more than what is needed.
- ☐ b. cheap.
- ☐ c. dry.
- ☐ d. stored in sacks.

_____

Add your scores for questions 1–6. Enter the total here and on the graph on page 215.   **Total Score**

_____

31 Sleep

Are you tired? Do you feel grouchy and less alert than usual? Do you often catch colds and flu? If so, you might consider changing your sleep habits. Good health demands good sleep. Studies have shown that most people need eight hours of sleep each day. Americans, however, on the average get only seven hours. One-third of us get just six hours. And good health is not simply a matter of how much sleep you get. It's also the type of sleep.

Non-rapid eye movement (NREM) sleep lets your body grow and repair itself. During NREM sleep, your muscles relax. Your heart rate and breathing rate decrease. Your eyes roll slowly back and forth; then they stop moving. Most of the sleeping you do is NREM sleep.

Rapid eye movement (REM) sleep restores your brain. During REM sleep, you dream. You may not remember every dream. But every time you sleep, you dream. Your eyes move back and forth quickly. Your breathing and heartbeat increase. Your muscles become paralyzed. About 25 percent of your sleep is REM sleep. You need enough of both kinds of sleep to be healthy.

Is it a real concern if you don't get enough good sleep? It certainly is. Poor sleep puts you and others at risk. More than 100,000 car accidents are caused each year by drivers who nod off. Almost $100 billion is lost yearly in the business and environmental sectors. People <u>deprived</u> of sleep have been factors in the *Challenger* space shuttle tragedy, the Exxon *Valdez* oil spill, and the Chernobyl nuclear reactor accident. So do yourself and everyone around you a favor. Don't cheat yourself out of good sleep!

Main Idea	1	Answer	Score
	Mark the *main idea*	M	15
	Mark the statement that is *too broad*	B	5
	Mark the statement that is *too narrow*	N	5

a. People don't get enough sleep.	☐	____
b. We dream during REM sleep.	☐	____
c. Everyone needs good sleep to be physically and mentally healthy.	☐	____

Score 15 points for each correct answer.   **Score**

Subject Matter **2** This passage is mainly about why
- ☐ a. people dream.
- ☐ b. muscles become paralyzed during sleep.
- ☐ c. people catch colds and the flu.
- ☐ d. people need good sleep.   _____

Supporting Details **3** Most nightly sleep is
- ☐ a. NREM sleep.
- ☐ b. REM sleep.
- ☐ c. sleep occurring between 1:00 and 3:00 A.M.
- ☐ d. sleep that restores your brain.   _____

Conclusion **4** "Good sleep" can be described as
- ☐ a. about eight hours of NREM and REM sleep.
- ☐ b. sleeping soundly when you're sick.
- ☐ c. several hours of rest each day.
- ☐ d. the time in which you dream.   _____

Clarifying Devices **5** To help the reader understand how business and the environment are affected by poor sleep habits, the writer
- ☐ a. lists facts in time order.
- ☐ b. compares and contrasts two accidents.
- ☐ c. lists several big accidents.
- ☐ d. uses transition words.   _____

Vocabulary in Context **6** In this passage deprived means
- ☐ a. permitted to.
- ☐ b. kept from having.
- ☐ c. enjoying.
- ☐ d. wishing to.   _____

Add your scores for questions 1–6. Enter the total here and on the graph on page 215.   **Total Score**   _____

32 "I Will Fight No More Forever"

For centuries the Nez Perce called Oregon's Wallowa Valley home. Then in 1876, the U.S. government ordered this Native American tribe to move to a reservation. A few bands rebelled. These groups began fighting two wars—one with the United States Army, the other with nature. The groups needed meat and hides for the coming winter. Stopping to hunt meant risking death at the hands of the pursuing army. Pushing on to the safety of the Canadian border meant death at the hands of nature.

The Nez Perce stopped to hunt on September 30, 1877. Before they could continue on to Canada, their pursuers caught up. They fought all day. When night fell, the Nez Perce dug shelter pits for the women and children. They dug rifle pits for the warriors. Snow fell for five days and nights. The Nez Perce huddled in their pits while rifle bullets and cannon shells rained down on them. On the afternoon of October 5, 1877, Chief Joseph and five warriors approached General Howard of the United States Army. After handing over his rifle, Joseph spoke:

"The little children are freezing to death. My people, some of them, have run away to the hills and have no blankets, no food. No one knows where they are—perhaps freezing to death. I want to have time to look for my children and see how many I can find. Maybe I shall find them among the dead. I am tired; my heart is sick and sad. From where the sun now stands, I will fight no more forever."

Joseph was speaking for the Nez Perce that afternoon, but he might have been speaking for all Native Americans. The United States government <u>mission</u> to confine the first Americans was now nearly over.

Main Idea	1		
		Answer	**Score**
	Mark the *main idea*	**M**	15
	Mark the statement that is *too broad*	**B**	5
	Mark the statement that is *too narrow*	**N**	5

a. The United States government had a harsh Indian policy. ☐ _____

b. The United States Army pursued the Nez Perce until the Nez Perce could no longer fight. ☐ _____

c. Chief Joseph surrendered to General Howard. ☐ _____

Subject Matter　　2　This passage is mainly about
- [ ] a. General Howard and the United States Army.
- [ ] b. the Canadians.
- [ ] c. the Nez Perce and Chief Joseph.
- [ ] d. all Native Americans.　　　　_____

Supporting Details　　3　The Nez Perce headed for the Canadian border because
- [ ] a. they were Canadian citizens.
- [ ] b. the hunting was better in Canada.
- [ ] c. they would be safe from the United States Army there.
- [ ] d. they liked the colder weather.　　　　_____

Conclusion　　4　What did Chief Joseph mean when he said, "I will fight no more forever?"
- [ ] a. The battle was just beginning.
- [ ] b. He would never again take part in such a battle.
- [ ] c. He would continue to fight forever.
- [ ] d. He would stop fighting until he reached Canada.　　　　_____

Clarifying Devices　　5　What does the phrase "rifle bullets and cannon shells rained down on them" tell about the attack?
- [ ] a. The army attack was continuous and heavy.
- [ ] b. The Nez Perce were getting very wet.
- [ ] c. The army attack did not harm anyone.
- [ ] d. The Nez Perce avoided the attack.　　　　_____

Vocabulary in Context　　6　In this passage the word <u>mission</u> means
- [ ] a. the headquarters of a religious group.
- [ ] b. something that is missing.
- [ ] c. an error in action or judgment.
- [ ] d. the task or job of a military unit.　　　　_____

Add your scores for questions 1–6. Enter the total here and on the graph on page 215.　　Total Score　　_____

33 Some Kinds of Poetry

You deal with poetry more than you probably think. It may not always be good poetry, but the words of many songs are poems. They use rhyme and strong images or pictures painted in words. You may also find poems on some greeting cards. The best of these will quote a poem from some well-known writer.

Generally we say that there are two kinds of poetry. These are the lyric poem and the narrative poem. A lyric is usually a short poem. It does not tell a story. Instead, it expresses some emotion. For example, a poet may write a lyric poem about getting his child to bed. He does not tell about everything that happens. But he may pick up one small part, such as tucking the child in. He may describe this in a line or two. Then he may go on to tell his thoughts and memories. Maybe he thinks of his other children when they were young. Maybe he remembers his own childhood. Expressing his feelings in verse, he writes a lyric poem.

Narrative poems are poems that tell stories. Some people find these easier to understand than lyric poems. There are many different types of narrative poems. For instance, you may know about ballads. These are often stories about unhappy love affairs. They can also be about characters such as Jesse James. Some are about tragedies such as the sinking of a ship. Ballads have a lot of action and dialogue. The rhyme in them is often also very strong.

Some narrative poems have little or no rhyme. One famous writer of narrative poems was Robert Frost. Frost lived on a farm in New England. Many of his narratives were about that life. Couples would argue. People would die. Their stories came to life in Frost's poems.

Main Idea	1		
		Answer	Score
	Mark the *main idea*	M	15
	Mark the statement that is *too broad*	B	5
	Mark the statement that is *too narrow*	N	5

a.	Lyric poems and narrative poems have different characteristics.	☐ ____
b.	There are various kinds of poems.	☐ ____
c.	Narrative poems tell stories.	☐ ____

Subject Matter   **2**   This passage is mainly about
- [ ] a. the stories that narrative poems tell.
- [ ] b. Robert Frost.
- [ ] c. differences between lyric and narrative poetry.
- [ ] d. poems that express emotion.   ____

Supporting Details   **3**   A ballad is a
- [ ] a. type of lyric poem.
- [ ] b. type of narrative poem.
- [ ] c. poem with no rhyme.
- [ ] d. poem about putting a child to bed.   ____

Conclusion   **4**   You can conclude from this passage that Robert Frost's narratives were mostly
- [ ] a. about everyday events.
- [ ] b. hard to understand.
- [ ] c. filled with exaggeration.
- [ ] d. ignored by most other poets.   ____

Clarifying Devices   **5**   The writer helps you understand what a lyric poem is by
- [ ] a. explaining what one might be about.
- [ ] b. quoting from a lyric poem.
- [ ] c. quoting a definition from a dictionary.
- [ ] d. giving a short history of lyrics.   ____

Vocabulary in Context   **6**   <u>Tragedies</u> are
- [ ] a. surprises.
- [ ] b. happy events.
- [ ] c. events involving ships.
- [ ] d. sad events.   ____

Add your scores for questions 1–6. Enter the total here and on the graph on page 215.   **Total Score**   ____

34 "Please Excuse My Dear Aunt Sally"

Some students are confused by math problems that contain parentheses. One example is the problem $3(4 + 1)^2 - 8$. What number does this equal? You probably know what the exponent 2 means. When you see that small 2 above the line, it means that a number should be multiplied by itself, or squared. But the problem has other steps in it. The 3 directly in front of the parentheses means you should multiply. The problem also contains addition and subtraction. What should you do first?

To help students grasp this kind of problem, a teacher will explain the order of operations. The steps must be done in a certain order.

To remember the order of the steps, you can use a memory trick. It is the key sentence "Please excuse my dear Aunt Sally." The first letters in the words are PEMDAS. They stand for parentheses, exponents, multiply, divide, add, subtract.

Let's apply the memory trick to the problem above. First do any math inside parentheses. Then use any exponents. Do any multiplying or dividing necessary. Then do any adding or subtracting. Follow the steps to see how this works.

- The math inside the **p**arentheses is to add $4 + 1$. When you do that step, the problem looks like this: $3(5)^2 - 8$
- Next, use the **e**xponent 2. That means multiply 5 by itself. You'll have this result: $3(25) - 8$
- Now **m**ultiply 3 times 25. You will come up with this: $75 - 8$
- **S**ubtract 8 from 75 and you're done: The answer is 67

Of course, this kind of memory <u>device</u> is useless if you can't remember the key sentence. Some students like to create their own sentences, such as "Purple elephants marching down a street." What similar memory device can you dream up?

Main Idea	1		Answer	Score
	Mark the *main idea*		**M**	15
	Mark the statement that is *too broad*		**B**	5
	Mark the statement that is *too narrow*		**N**	5
	a. Math problems can be confusing.		☐	___
	b. The first step in many problems is to do the math that's in parentheses.		☐	___
	c. A memory trick can help you remember the order of operations.		☐	___

Subject Matter   **2**   This passage is mainly about

☐ a. doing math problems in the right order.

☐ b. making up your own memory tricks.

☐ c. using exponents in math problems.

☐ d. learning how to multiply.   _____

Supporting   **3**   The fourth and fifth words in "Please excuse my
Details   dear Aunt Sally" remind you to

☐ a. add before you divide.

☐ b. use exponents before you divide.

☐ c. divide before you add.

☐ d. multiply before you divide.   _____

Conclusion   **4**   The last paragraph of the passage is intended to

☐ a. convince you math is easy.

☐ b. make you angry.

☐ c. amuse you.

☐ d. remind you to check your answers to
math problems.   _____

Clarifying   **5**   The purpose of the bulleted list in the passage is to
Devices

☐ a. introduce the topic.

☐ b. help you understand how to do the problem
in the right order.

☐ c. define words like *exponent.*

☐ d. teach you how to multiply.   _____

Vocabulary   **6**   In this passage the word <u>device</u> means
in Context

☐ a. to create or make.

☐ b. a loud noise.

☐ c. an adding machine.

☐ d. an aid or tool.   _____

Add your scores for questions 1–6. Enter the total here   **Total**
and on the graph on page 215.   **Score**   _____

35 Seed Plants

What plants do you see in your neighborhood? Trees such as maple and ginkgo and flowers such as geraniums and columbines are possibilities. Fruits and crops such as strawberries, pumpkins, and corn may grow in some gardens. You're also likely to see grass and weeds. All these plants, and most others we see, are seed plants. Seed plants—plants grown from seeds—need water, sunlight, and minerals to thrive.

All seed plants have three main parts: roots, stems, and leaves; some seed plants also have flowers. Each part of a plant is essential for its continuing development. Roots grow downward into the soil or toward water. As the roots branch out throughout the soil, they <u>absorb</u> water and minerals. The roots of some plants also store food to help the plants survive the winter. Roots act as an anchor, holding the plant firmly in the soil.

Most stems grow above ground. Some seed plants, however, have special stems that grow underground. For example, onions and tulips have bulbs, which are stem parts that grow underground. Stems have tubes that carry food, water, and minerals throughout the plant. Stems also grow leaves and hold them up toward sunlight. Green plants use energy from the sun to make food through photosynthesis, which takes place in the leaves and sometimes in the stems of seed plants.

Seed plants form seeds to reproduce new plants. Some form seeds, such as pine cones and acorns, on branches of leaves. Other plants have flowers that make seeds inside a fruit, such as apples and cucumbers. The seeds of all plants grow into new plants, many of which play important roles in our lives. Wood, rubber, medicines, dyes, cloth fibers, and cooking oils all come from seed plants. Most importantly, we depend on seed plants as sources of food for animals and for ourselves.

Main Idea	1	Answer	Score
	Mark the *main idea*	M	15
	Mark the statement that is *too broad*	B	5
	Mark the statement that is *too narrow*	N	5
	a. Most plants are seed plants.	☐	___
	b. Some seed plants have flowers as well as roots, stems, and leaves.	☐	___
	c. Seed plants have many parts and can serve many purposes.	☐	___

Subject Matter   2   The purpose of this passage is to
- [ ] a. give a history of seed plants.
- [ ] b. describe the parts of seed plants and their purposes.
- [ ] c. compare seed plants and seedless plants.
- [ ] d. describe several uses of seed plants.   _____

Supporting Details   3   The roots of a seed plant
- [ ] a. hold the plant in the ground.
- [ ] b. grow above ground and develop leaves.
- [ ] c. are important for photosynthesis.
- [ ] d. reproduce new plants by forming seeds.   _____

Conclusion   4   After reading this passage, we can conclude that
- [ ] a. seed plants do not need seeds to reproduce.
- [ ] b. green plants will thrive in areas with little sunlight and water.
- [ ] c. photosynthesis happens only at night.
- [ ] d. human life is dependent on seed plants.   _____

Clarifying Devices   5   To make the point that some seed plants have special stems that grow underground, the author
- [ ] a. describes places where these plants grow.
- [ ] b. tells some uses of seed plants.
- [ ] c. uses the example of plants with bulbs.
- [ ] d. uses the example of flowers that make seeds inside a fruit.   _____

Vocabulary in Context   6   To absorb means to
- [ ] a. grow and live.
- [ ] b. suck up and take in.
- [ ] c. want and need.
- [ ] d. carry and use.   _____

Add your scores for questions 1–6. Enter the total here and on the graph on page 215.   Total Score   _____

36 What Is Sociology?

Sociology is the study of people in groups. The scientists who study people are called sociologists. They study people in small groups. These may be families. They study people in larger groups. These may be towns or cities. Sometimes they even study people in very large groups such as whole nations. They try to make sense of human behavior.

Sociologists study the various things that cause groups to form and what happens in the groups. For instance, they may look at ethnic groups and the things that people in them do. They may look at behavior in various social classes. They may study the way organizations work. They examine work places. They analyze schools. They look at crime and its causes. They study how groups stay the same. They also study how groups change.

Often sociologists look at the same things other social scientists look at. For instance, sociologists study groups during elections. They ask why a group chooses a candidate. Political scientists study the same group. But they look at something different. They look for voting patterns.

How do sociologists study groups? One way is to make a <u>model</u>. The model is a theory. It tries to explain all societies. Sociologists might look at families. They will try to find a pattern. The pattern helps them to explain all groups.

Another way to study groups is to collect information about them. Sociologists use surveys. They ask questions. They look at statistics. They do scientific research.

Sociology is part of daily life. We know our place in a group. We know who is in our group. We know its rules. Our groups vary in size. Lunching with a friend makes a group. A big crowd is a group. Sociologists want to know how groups affect our lives.

Main Idea   1 —————————————————————————————

	Answer	Score
Mark the *main idea*	**M**	15
Mark the statement that is *too broad*	**B**	5
Mark the statement that is *too narrow*	**N**	5

a. Sociology is the scientific study of people in groups. ☐ _____

b. Sociology is one of the social studies. ☐ _____

c. Sociologists may study groups by collecting information about them. ☐ _____

Subject Matter 2 This passage is mostly about
- ☐ a. families.
- ☐ b. the training sociologists get.
- ☐ c. why people in groups often don't get along.
- ☐ d. what sociologists do.

_____

Supporting Details 3 Which of the following statements is true?
- ☐ a. Sociologists choose candidates for elections.
- ☐ b. Sociologists look at how groups change.
- ☐ c. Sociologists only study families.
- ☐ d. Sociologists have found no patterns among groups.

_____

Conclusion 4 The writer of the passage leads you to believe that
- ☐ a. sociology is a hard career to train for.
- ☐ b. human behavior cannot be explained by scientists.
- ☐ c. sociologists are satisfied with making models of groups.
- ☐ d. much of what you do in your life is part of a group.

_____

Clarifying Devices 5 The writer discusses political scientists to show
- ☐ a. how they are different from sociologists.
- ☐ b. that they work harder than sociologists.
- ☐ c. that they and sociologists get similar training.
- ☐ d. that only political scientists create models.

_____

Vocabulary in Context 6 The word <u>model</u> in this passage means a
- ☐ a. theory that describes a process.
- ☐ b. person who poses for photographers.
- ☐ c. small copy of something.
- ☐ d. list of questions.

_____

Add your scores for questions 1–6. Enter the total here and on the graph on page 215.

Total Score

_____

37 Religious Theater?

Imagine that you live in the Middle Ages—say around 1450. There are no cars or trains. There are no televisions or electric lights. You work long hours on your farm or in your shop. So what do you do when you want to have a little fun?

For one thing, you might see a play. Most plays of that time were based on religious topics. Called miracle plays, they dealt with lives of saints or stories from the Bible. At first they were put on in churches. But times changed. The plays went out of the churches and into the streets. And they changed from religious into <u>secular</u> shows.

Imagine yourself in this era. Here is what might happen. A crier might come through your town several days in advance, announcing that a theater troop would soon arrive. These troops traveled from one location to another with a series of wheeled platforms. Each platform presented a different scene from a play, and they were wheeled along in succession. This time the play might be about John the Baptist. He was beheaded at the request of King Herod's daughter Salome. You might be treated to Salome's sensual dance before Herod's guests. You might hear Herod's promise to give her anything she wanted. The beheading scene would be full of fake blood and gore, with a dummy replacing the actor at just the right moment. Blood and violence were favorites of the audiences. They enlivened most "religious" performances.

Some of the staging of these performances was amazing. Christ was raised from his tomb by weights and pulleys. A trapdoor represented the opening and closing mouth of Hell. Fork-tailed devils, their bodies covered with horsehair, ran out into the audience and frightened people. A lesson about what happens to evil folks might have been in there somewhere. But mostly these shows were pure entertainment.

Main Idea	1		
		Answer	Score
	Mark the *main idea*	**M**	15
	Mark the statement that is *too broad*	**B**	5
	Mark the statement that is *too narrow*	**N**	5

a. The scenery at a play in the Middle Ages was often very complicated. ☐ _____

b. People in the Middle Ages loved plays. ☐ _____

c. In the Middle Ages, so-called religious plays were often not very religious. ☐ _____

Subject Matter	**2**	This passage deals mostly with
		☐ a. the history of religious theater.
		☐ b. the content and staging of plays in the Middle Ages.
		☐ c. what audiences thought about religious plays.
		☐ d. why actors in the Middle Ages wore masks. _____

Supporting Details	**3**	Most people of the period saw plays
		☐ a. in theaters.
		☐ b. in churches.
		☐ c. on platforms wheeled into towns.
		☐ d. in castles. _____

Conclusion	**4**	When watching these plays, most members of the audience probably
		☐ a. felt bored.
		☐ b. said their prayers.
		☐ c. felt happy and amused.
		☐ d. got angry with their neighbors. _____

Clarifying Devices	**5**	In the second paragraph, the word *But* signals a
		☐ a. contrast.
		☐ b. choice.
		☐ c. description.
		☐ d. story in time order. _____

Vocabulary in Context	**6**	In this passage secular means
		☐ a. religious.
		☐ b. not religious.
		☐ c. true to life.
		☐ d. having many actors. _____

Add your scores for questions 1–6. Enter the total here and on the graph on page 215.   **Total Score**   _____

38 The Oldest Math Puzzle

As I was going to St. Ives, I met a man with seven wives.
Every wife had seven sacks, and every sack had seven cats.
Cats, sacks, men, and wives, how many were going to St. Ives?

The *Guinness Book of World Records* tells us that this is the oldest math puzzle. Versions of it have been found as early as 1650 B.C. Of course, the very old versions were not in English. Also, the problem may have other objects. Every wife could have seven baskets, with seven eggs in each basket. But the key idea of the puzzle remains the same in all the versions.

Most people are tricked by the puzzle for this reason. They start solving it too quickly. They begin multiplying and adding, trying to compute the total number of people and things described. They make a very common math mistake—they do not answer the question. The question asks only how many are going to St. Ives. If you read the puzzle again, you'll see that only one person, the person speaking, is definitely going to St. Ives. The man with the <u>multiplicity</u> of wives, sacks, and cats might be going the opposite direction. He might not be going anywhere at all.

Here is another example. A typical textbook problem might describe a worker packing books in boxes. There are 86 books. He puts 10 books in a box. How many boxes does he need? Dividing 86 by 10 gives the answer 8.6. But that is not the answer to the question. You can't have 8.6 boxes. The answer to the question in the problem is 9 boxes. It is not 8.6 boxes.

The next time you are working a math problem, remember the man going to St. Ives. Be sure you aren't tricked. Read the problem a final time and check that you have answered the correct question.

Main Idea	1		
		Answer	**Score**
Mark the *main idea*		M	15
Mark the statement that is *too broad*		B	5
Mark the statement that is *too narrow*		N	5

a. Be careful to answer the correct question in a math problem. ☐ ____

b. Many math puzzles are thousands of years old. ☐ ____

c. There's no such thing as 8.6 boxes. ☐ ____

Subject Matter   **2**   Which of these is another good title for the passage?
- ☐ a. Traveling to St. Ives
- ☐ b. Using Memory Tricks
- ☐ c. What's the Question?
- ☐ d. Using Multiplication   ____

Supporting Details   **3**   The person going to St. Ives
- ☐ a. is the speaker in the puzzle.
- ☐ b. has seven wives.
- ☐ c. carries a sack.
- ☐ d. likes to do math problems.   ____

Conclusion   **4**   Which of these statements is a conclusion the author wants you to draw?
- ☐ a. Sometimes math is a matter of common sense.
- ☐ b. Old puzzles are usually easy to figure out.
- ☐ c. Textbooks try to trick students
- ☐ d. St. Ives no longer exists.   ____

Clarifying Devices   **5**   The first three lines of this passage are in *italic type* to
- ☐ a. help you do the math in them.
- ☐ b. make them stand out from the regular text.
- ☐ c. indicate that you should read them twice.
- ☐ d. indicate that you should memorize them.   ____

Vocabulary in Context   **6**   In this passage the word multiplicity means
- ☐ a. the answer to a multiplication problem.
- ☐ b. the opposite of long division.
- ☐ c. a great many.
- ☐ d. the wrong number.   ____

Add your scores for questions 1–6. Enter the total here and on the graph on page 215.   **Total Score**   ____

39 Lights in the Night Sky

Look into the sky on a clear night, away from city lights. What do you see? Your eyes are dazzled by thousands of points of lights. Some of the lights twinkle; others glow steadily. The twinkling points of lights are stars, or large balls of very hot gases such as hydrogen, helium, iron, and calcium. The gases cause nuclear reactions inside the stars. The nuclear reactions release energy in the forms of light and heat. On a clear night, you can see as many as 2,500 stars with the naked eye. The points of light that have a steady glow are planets, most likely Venus, Mars, Jupiter, or Saturn. The difference between stars and planets in the sky is that stars give off their own light. The brightness of planets is caused by light reflected from the sun.

Some stars are isolated in the sky; others are grouped into clusters. Stars and star clusters are grouped into even larger groups called galaxies. There are tens of millions of galaxies in the universe. Our galaxy, the Milky Way, contains more than 100 billion stars. The universe contains more than a billion billion stars. Each star has its own position in space. That's why we know where to look in the sky for individual stars, such as Polaris, and for arrangements of stars, such as the Big Dipper.

Though stars look small, they actually are quite large. A star can range in size from thousands to millions of miles across. Most stars only look small because they are so far away from Earth. Distance also plays a role in a star's brightness when viewed from Earth. The larger and hotter the star, the brighter it is. But two stars of the same size and temperature will not appear to have the same brightness if they are at different distances from Earth. The star farther away from Earth will seem dimmer than the one that is closer. The very closest star to Earth is the sun.

Main Idea	1		
		Answer	**Score**
	Mark the *main idea*	M	15
	Mark the statement that is *too broad*	B	5
	Mark the statement that is *too narrow*	N	5

a. Stars, huge balls of hot gases, can be found by the billions in our universe. ☐ _____

b. There are thousands of bright lights in the night sky. ☐ _____

c. Every star has its own particular position in the sky. ☐ _____

Subject Matter   **2**   This passage is mostly concerned with
- ☐ a. stars.
- ☐ b. light energy.
- ☐ c. galaxies.
- ☐ d. planets.

_____

Supporting Details   **3**   The Milky Way is a
- ☐ a. star.
- ☐ b. universe.
- ☐ c. galaxy.
- ☐ d. star cluster.

_____

Conclusion   **4**   The author's conclusion that the sun is Earth's nearest star is
- ☐ a. incorrect because the sun is a planet similar to Earth.
- ☐ b. correct because authors never mislead their readers.
- ☐ c. incorrect because no star is as hot as the sun.
- ☐ d. correct because the sun gives off light and heat and is the largest visible point of light.

_____

Clarifying Devices   **5**   The first paragraph of this passage does **not** include
- ☐ a. a definition of a star.
- ☐ b. the names of several bodies in the night sky.
- ☐ c. facts about the size of stars.
- ☐ d. a comparison between stars and planets.

_____

Vocabulary in Context   **6**   To be <u>isolated</u> means to be
- ☐ a. together in a group.
- ☐ b. set apart from others.
- ☐ c. twinkling and sparkling.
- ☐ d. in a set position in space.

_____

Add your scores for questions 1–6. Enter the total here and on the graph on page 215.   **Total Score**

_____

40 Tropical Rain Forests

Perhaps you have not stepped into a tropical rain forest. Perhaps you have not felt its year-round temperatures of 70 to 80 degrees. Perhaps you have not gotten wet in downpours that bring more than 80 inches of rain each year. Perhaps you have not looked up to see a green canopy of leaves that blocks the blue of the sky. Perhaps you have never been there. But the tropical rain forest has come to you.

When you smell coffee, eat a banana, or sprinkle cinnamon on your toast, the rain forest comes to you. Coffee beans, bananas, and cinnamon, along with pine-apple, mangoes, and chocolate, are all from the tropical rain forest. Even your chewing gum has its origins there. Chicle, the basis for gum, comes from a rain forest tree.

Tropical rain forests are found in lands near the equator, such as Brazil and Malaysia. They cover about two percent of the earth's surface.

Many medicines are made from plants that grow in the tropical rain forest. These include drugs for headaches, high blood pressure, and heart disease. Researchers think there may be many more remedies in the plants there.

The tropical rain forest holds much of Earth's biological diversity. It has three-fourths of all known species of plants and animals. As many as 30 million different kinds of insects live there too.

But the earth is losing its rain forests. Trees are cut for their lumber. Land is cleared by fire to make way for crops and cattle. An area about the size of West Virginia is deforested each year. When the trees are gone, the plants are gone. The animals will be gone too. Many people are concerned. They believe that the survival of the rain forest is crucial to the survival of our world.

Main Idea 1

	Answer	Score
Mark the *main idea*	M	15
Mark the statement that is *too broad*	B	5
Mark the statement that is *too narrow*	N	5

a. Much rain forest land is being deforested each year. ☐ _____

b. Rain forests are interesting places. ☐ _____

c. Tropical rain forests are important to people and the earth. ☐ _____

Score 15 points for each correct answer. Score

Subject Matter   **2**   This passage is primarily
- ☐ a. an informative article about rain forests.
- ☐ b. a personal narrative about one person's trip to a rain forest.
- ☐ c. a description of the rain forest in Brazil.
- ☐ d. the history of rain forests. _____

Supporting Details   **3**   Rain forests are located
- ☐ a. close to deserts.
- ☐ b. near the equator.
- ☐ c. near the South Pole.
- ☐ d. in isolated mountain regions. _____

Conclusion   **4**   The last paragraph suggests that
- ☐ a. lumber and cattle come from rain forests.
- ☐ b. there is no hope for rain forests because the trees, plants, and animals are gone.
- ☐ c. West Virginia is a rain forest.
- ☐ d. we will be in trouble if we lose the rain forests. _____

Clarifying Devices   **5**   The writer attempts to involve the reader in the first two paragraphs by
- ☐ a. frequently using the word *you.*
- ☐ b. writing from the first-person point of view.
- ☐ c. using many convincing numbers and facts.
- ☐ d. asking the reader many questions. _____

Vocabulary in Context   **6**   <u>Diversity</u> means
- ☐ a. area.
- ☐ b. variety.
- ☐ c. desert.
- ☐ d. rain water. _____

Add your scores for questions 1–6. Enter the total here and on the graph on page 215.   Total Score _____

41 Bluegrass

There are many types of music known as American. These include jazz, blues, and Dixieland. One of the newer American music forms is bluegrass. It was developed in the 1930s and '40s, mostly through the work of band leader Bill Monroe.

Monroe was born in Kentucky in 1911. When he began to put together a band, he named it the Blue Grass Boys, after his home state.

In certain ways, Monroe's music developed from country music. It used many of the same instruments: banjo, fiddle, and guitar. But Monroe was looking for a different sound. For one thing, he played the mandolin. This is a stringed instrument that was not often heard in country music then. Monroe would tune his mandolin up to match the notes played by his fiddlers. When his band did vocals, it would be at this same high pitch. And they would always play very fast.

Monroe played with many musicians over the years. The music of his band would adjust to new players' styles. For example, a jug player or an accordionist could change the band's sound. By the mid-1940s Monroe had his <u>premier</u> band. He played the mandolin, while other members played the fiddle and the bass. One important member was banjo player Earl Scruggs. Scruggs had a distinctive playing style, picking the banjo with three fingers rather than two. This created a strong, even flow of sound. Guitar player Lester Flatt also had a unique picking style.

The new banjo and guitar styles put the finishing touches on the band's music. Together with the high pitch and the fast playing, Monroe had created a new sound. Soon others began to copy it. The style of music became known as bluegrass, named after Monroe's band. Today bluegrass playing can be heard all over the country.

Main Idea	1		
		Answer	**Score**
	Mark the *main idea*	M	15
	Mark the statement that is *too broad*	B	5
	Mark the statement that is *too narrow*	N	5

a. Bill Monroe originated the style of music known as bluegrass. ☐ _____

b. Earl Scruggs picked a banjo with three fingers. ☐ _____

c. There are many types of American music. ☐ _____

Score 15 points for each correct answer.   **Score**

Subject Matter   **2**   This passage is mostly concerned with
- ☐ a. battles between Monroe and Scruggs.
- ☐ b. how bluegrass music developed.
- ☐ c. differences between jazz and bluegrass.
- ☐ d. different styles of playing the banjo.   ____

Supporting Details   **3**   Bill Monroe played the
- ☐ a. violin.
- ☐ b. mandolin.
- ☐ c. guitar.
- ☐ d. banjo.   ____

Conclusion   **4**   You can tell that Monroe
- ☐ a. knew exactly how he wanted bluegrass to sound from the very beginning.
- ☐ b. had certain ideas about bluegrass, but was content to let it develop.
- ☐ c. wanted to control everything his musicians played.
- ☐ d. wanted to play only in Kentucky.   ____

Clarifying Devices   **5**   The term "finishing touches" in the final paragraph refers to
- ☐ a. a hands-on guitar playing style.
- ☐ b. the end of something.
- ☐ c. elements that make something complete.
- ☐ d. very special kinds of varnish.   ____

Vocabulary in Context   **6**   In this passage <u>premier</u> means
- ☐ a. opening night at a movie.
- ☐ b. a government leader.
- ☐ c. the very worst.
- ☐ d. first in ranking.   ____

Add your scores for questions 1–6. Enter the total here and on the graph on page 215.   **Total Score**   ____

42 Four Out of Five Doctors Recommend . . .

You have probably seen many advertisements for medicines. The ads try to convince you to buy the medicine. They may say, for example, that four out of five doctors recommend a particular headache product. What does this really mean? Exactly how many doctors like the headache medicine? To understand the math behind advertising <u>claims</u> like these, you need to think about how fractions work.

Let's say 500 doctors are in a survey, and 400 of them like the medicine. Then the fraction $\frac{400}{500}$ shows what part of the whole group recommends the product. This fraction is equal to $\frac{4}{5}$. But so are the fractions $\frac{400}{500}$ and $\frac{4000}{5000}$ and even $\frac{40000}{50000}$. So you can't really tell how many doctors were questioned in the survey. All you know is that four out of five said the medicine was good.

So why don't they tell you how many doctors were asked? They could say, "We asked 500 doctors, and 400 of them say the medicine is great." But they don't. Instead they write, "Four out of five doctors recommend our medicine." You aren't told the actual number of doctors in the survey. Maybe they only asked 50. But by telling you four out of five, they may hope you will think that *thousands* of doctors were questioned.

Next time you see an ad that tells you four out of five doctors like a medicine, stop and guess how many doctors that is. You might even write a letter to find out the actual number.

Main Idea 1		Answer	Score
Mark the *main idea*		M	15
Mark the statement that is *too broad*		B	5
Mark the statement that is *too narrow*		N	5

a. Advertisers use numbers like "four out of five" to mislead people.	☐	_____
a. The fraction $\frac{40}{50}$ is equal to $\frac{4}{5}$.	☐	_____
c. Fractions are sometimes confusing.	☐	_____

Subject Matter   **2**   Another good title for this passage is
- ☐ a. Reading Labels on Medicine Bottles.
- ☐ b. Why Doctors Recommend Certain Medicines.
- ☐ c. Fractions Always Tell the Truth.
- ☐ d. How Fractions Are Used in Advertising.   _____

Supporting Details   **3**   A statement like "four out of five"
- ☐ a. always means 40 out of 50 people.
- ☐ b. doesn't tell exactly how many people were counted.
- ☐ c. is the fairest way to explain a survey.
- ☐ d. should convince you to buy certain medicines.   _____

Conclusion   **4**   The author of this passage thinks you should
- ☐ a. think carefully about ads you hear.
- ☐ b. realize that all ads are full of lies.
- ☐ c. get better at doing math.
- ☐ d. realize that advertisers don't want to mislead people.   _____

Clarifying Devices   **5**   The final paragraph of the passage is intended as a
- ☐ a. criticism of people who don't write letters.
- ☐ b. comparison.
- ☐ c. recommendation.
- ☐ d. joke.   _____

Vocabulary in Context   **6**   In this passage the word <u>claims</u> means
- ☐ a. statements that something is true.
- ☐ b. fractions.
- ☐ c. pieces of land belonging to a person.
- ☐ d. lies.   _____

Add your scores for questions 1–6. Enter the total here and on the graph on page 215.   **Total Score**   _____

43 The Basics of Weather

The alarm clock rings. You turn on the radio to hear the weather report. Why? Weather affects everything in our lives. It affects what we wear and the activities we perform. It affects the crops we grow and the work we do. But what *is* weather? It is what's happening in the atmosphere, that thick layer of air that surrounds the earth. Air temperature, wind, precipitation, and clouds work together to create weather.

The sun has a great effect on weather. Why? The sun warms the surface of the earth. Some parts of land warm faster than others. A parking lot, for instance, absorbs the sun's heat more quickly than a forest. All land, however, absorbs the sun's heat faster than a body of water. A forest, therefore, warms more quickly than a large lake or ocean. The warmed land and water give off heat to the air above them. The hot air rises, and as it <u>ascends</u>, cooler air moves in to replace it. This movement of air is called wind.

The sun's heat also causes water from land, oceans, and lakes to evaporate into the air. Other water vapor, or gas, is released into the air from plants, animals, and people. As water vapor rises in the air, it cools and forms drops of water. The drops of water form clouds. Inside a cloud, the drops join together, becoming larger and larger. When they get too big and heavy, they fall as precipitation. Rain is the most common form of precipitation. But when the air in and below a cloud is cold enough, the precipitation may fall as sleet, hail, or snow.

Clouds affect air temperature as well as precipitation. Clouds keep some of the sun's heat from reaching the earth. On a mostly cloudy day, less of the sun's heat reaches the earth. So when the weather report predicts a mostly cloudy day, consider dressing a tad warmer.

Main Idea	1		Answer	Score
	Mark the *main idea*		M	15
	Mark the statement that is *too broad*		B	5
	Mark the statement that is *too narrow*		N	5
	a. Hot air rises.		☐	_____
	b. Weather is in the atmosphere.		☐	_____
	c. Temperature, wind, precipitation, and clouds work together to create weather.		☐	_____

Subject Matter   **2**   Another good title for this passage is
- ☐ a. Weather: A Combination of Factors.
- ☐ b. Radio and the Weather.
- ☐ c. Keep That Sweater Handy.
- ☐ d. Weather Extremes: Why They Happen.   _____

Supporting Details   **3**   The most important fact about the sun in this passage is that it
- ☐ a. is the center of our universe.
- ☐ b. radiates sunshine to all the planets and stars.
- ☐ c. warms the earth and causes water to evaporate.
- ☐ d. hides behind clouds in the sky.   _____

Conclusion   **4**   It is clear that
- ☐ a. early risers listen to weather reports.
- ☐ b. precipitation makes clouds in the sky.
- ☐ c. weather forecasters should be more accurate.
- ☐ d. weather would not happen if the sun were cold.   _____

Clarifying Devices   **5**   To help show that surfaces absorb heat at different rates, the author uses
- ☐ a. strong arguments.
- ☐ b. a brief story.
- ☐ c. examples.
- ☐ d. measurements.   _____

Vocabulary in Context   **6**   <u>Ascends</u> means
- ☐ a. goes down.
- ☐ b. goes up.
- ☐ c. goes from north to south.
- ☐ d. goes in a circle.   _____

Add your scores for questions 1–6. Enter the total here and on the graph on page 215.   **Total Score**   _____

44 An Earthquake's Effect on Japan

At dawn on January 17, 1995, the city of Kobe (KOH bee) was rocked by earthquake <u>tremors</u>. The worst tremor reached 7.2 on the Richter scale. Kobe is Japan's sixth largest city. It is also one of the world's largest ports. Within minutes, Kobe was a disaster area.

How bad was the damage? The earthquake was the worst to hit Japan in 72 years. There were more than 6,000 people dead. More than 35,000 were injured, and nearly 310,000 were left homeless. Some 75,000 buildings were damaged or destroyed. Total damage was estimated at $90 billion.

Were the Japanese prepared for earthquakes? They thought they were. They were expecting a big earthquake to strike one of their major cities. But they did not know when, where, or how big the earthquake would be. Architects and engineers believed they had designed earthquake-proof buildings, transportation, and public services. Kobe's few minutes of earth tremors shattered that belief.

What did people learn from the Kobe earthquake? What happened in Kobe suggests that earthquake hazard was not taken seriously enough. Some people believe that more can be done to reduce damage. They propose the following. More work should be put into quake-proofing buildings. Walls should be built to protect towns on the coast from large waves. Providers of emergency services must be better trained and better prepared. Citizens must be better educated on what to do when an earthquake strikes.

The major barrier to doing more is cost. Japan finds itself trying to balance the cost against the risk of a strong earthquake.

Main Idea   1

	Answer	Score
Mark the *main idea*	M	15
Mark the statement that is *too broad*	B	5
Mark the statement that is *too narrow*	N	5

a. There are lessons to be learned from the Kobe earthquake. ☐ _____

b. The earthquake in Kobe damaged about 75,000 buildings. ☐ _____

c. Japan has severe earthquakes. ☐ _____

Subject Matter **2** Which sentence best tells what this passage says?
- [ ] a. Cities can be made earthquake proof.
- [ ] b. More can be done to reduce the damage of earthquakes.
- [ ] c. Earthquakes do not do much damage.
- [ ] d. Nothing can be done to reduce the damage of earthquakes.

_____

Supporting Details **3** How many people died in the Kobe earthquake?
- [ ] a. more than 6,000
- [ ] b. about 90 billion
- [ ] c. nearly 310,000
- [ ] d. 72

_____

Conclusion **4** Why is more not done to protect cities from earthquakes?
- [ ] a. There never will be another earthquake.
- [ ] b. Engineers do not have the knowledge.
- [ ] c. Protection is very costly.
- [ ] d. No one takes earthquakes seriously.

_____

Clarifying Devices **5** The pattern used to develop this passage is
- [ ] a. chronological order.
- [ ] b. personal narrative.
- [ ] c. comparison and contrast.
- [ ] d. question and answer.

_____

Vocabulary in Context **6** Tremors are
- [ ] a. long, narrow ditches.
- [ ] b. shakings.
- [ ] c. claps of thunder.
- [ ] d. sirens.

_____

Add your scores for questions 1–6. Enter the total here and on the graph on page 215. **Total Score**

_____

45 Not All Pyramids are Square

The Pyramids of Egypt are one of the wonders of the world. Even today no one knows how these impressive monuments were constructed. The Great Pyramid is particularly striking. It is 480 feet high. The base is a square that is 756 feet on each side. It may have taken 4,000 workers 30 years to build this huge structure.

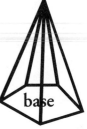

Many people think that all pyramids must look like the ones in Egypt. But that is not the case. Pyramids can have many different shapes. The side faces of a pyramid are always triangles. But the base can be some shape other than a square. The base can be a triangle. It can also be a five-sided shape called a pentagon or a six-sided shape called a hexagon. In fact, the base of a pyramid can be any <u>polygon</u>.

Pyramids are named by the shapes of their bases. The Egyptian pyramids are called square pyramids because their bases are squares. A triangular pyramid has a triangle for a base. A rectangular pyramid has a base that is a rectangle. So, the Egyptian pyramids are square. But many other pyramids aren't.

Models of pyramids are easy to make. Start by drawing any straight-sided shape. Put triangles on each side. Make each triangle the same height. Cut out the pattern and fold it up. You'll have a model of a pyramid. The drawing at the right shows a rectangle with four triangles around it. When folded, the pattern will make a rectangular pyramid.

Main Idea	1		Answer	Score
	Mark the *main idea*		M	15
	Mark the statement that is *too broad*		B	5
	Mark the statement that is *too narrow*		N	5

a. The Great Pyramid of Egypt has a square base. ☐ _____

b. Pyramids are named by the shapes of their bases. ☐ _____

c. Pyramids may be huge structures. ☐ _____

Subject Matter   **2**   This passage is mostly concerned with
- [ ] a. how long it took to build the Great Pyramid.
- [ ] b. the dimensions of the Great Pyramid.
- [ ] c. how different types of pyramids are named.
- [ ] d. comparing pyramids to squares and cubes.   _____

Supporting Details   **3**   The side faces of a pyramid
- [ ] a. are identical.
- [ ] b. are always triangles.
- [ ] c. are always squares.
- [ ] d. can be different shapes.   _____

Conclusion   **4**   The pyramid in the first diagram is a
- [ ] a. triangular pyramid.
- [ ] b. square pyramid.
- [ ] c. pentagonal pyramid.
- [ ] d. hexagonal pyramid.   _____

Clarifying Devices   **5**   The last paragraph helps you understand pyramids by
- [ ] a. describing the base and side faces.
- [ ] b. comparing them to the pyramids in Egypt.
- [ ] c. explaining how pyramids are named.
- [ ] d. showing you how to build a model.   _____

Vocabulary in Context   **6**   In this passage the word <u>polygon</u> means
- [ ] a. a flat shape with straight sides.
- [ ] b. a pyramid.
- [ ] c. an Egyptian temple.
- [ ] d. a pattern that can be folded into a pyramid.   _____

Add your scores for questions 1–6. Enter the total here and on the graph on page 215.   **Total Score**   _____

46 Novels Then and Now

Do you like to read novels? Many people do. Would it surprise you to know that novels are a rather new thing? They didn't exist until a few hundred years ago.

Some people say that the first novel was Cervantes' *Don Quixote* (kee HO tay). This Spanish story of a knight and his servant was written in the early 1600s. The two go from one adventure to another. The book follows their progress.

Modern novels usually have a more continuous story than *Don Quixote.* And their characters are more realistic. Novels of this sort did not appear until about 1740. At that time English writer Samuel Richardson published *Pamela.* This novel is about a young servant woman. The son of her employer tries to seduce her, but she does not give in. After *Pamela* many other novels were quickly published. Henry Fielding's *Tom Jones* tells of a young man who does not know who his parents are. His adventures paint a clear picture of English life at that time. Another early novel is *Robinson Crusoe* by Daniel Dafoe. It is about a man alone on a desert island.

Today there are many kinds of novels to choose from. In detective novels the hero is an investigator who solves a crime. Some of the earliest stories of this type were about Sherlock Holmes. But now there are many others. Author P. D. James writes about Adam Dalgleish. John D. McDonald wrote about Travis McGee.

Another type is the historical novel. In this kind of novel, made-up characters are placed in a real historical setting. It may be the Civil War, as in Margaret Mitchell's *Gone with the Wind.* It may even be the Stone Age.

Especially popular are Gothic novels. These are tales of terror with <u>eerie</u> settings and moods. A well-known modern Gothic writer is Stephen King.

Main Idea	1	Answer	Score
	Mark the *main idea*	**M**	15
	Mark the statement that is *too broad*	**B**	5
	Mark the statement that is *too narrow*	**N**	5

a.	Some early detective novels were about Sherlock Holmes.	☐ ____
b.	Reading novels is a popular form of entertainment.	☐ ____
c.	Novels have developed from the 1600s to the present time.	☐ ____

Subject Matter   **2**   Another good title for this passage would be
       ☐ a. What Made English Novels Popular.
       ☐ b. A Short History of the Novel.
       ☐ c. Types of Modern Novels.
       ☐ d. The First Novel.   _____

Supporting   **3**   Novels set in an atmosphere filled with fear and
Details   terror are called
       ☐ a. historical novels.
       ☐ b. adventure novels.
       ☐ c. detective novels.
       ☐ d. Gothic novels.   _____

Conclusion   **4**   We can conclude from this passage that Travis
McGee was
       ☐ a. a character who investigated crimes.
       ☐ b. the hero in *Gone with the Wind.*
       ☐ c. a real person.
       ☐ d. a character similar to Tom Jones.   _____

Clarifying   **5**   The author presents information in this passage
Devices   ☐ a. from the past to the present.
       ☐ b. from the present to the past.
       ☐ c. in order of importance.
       ☐ d. by describing the setting of each novel.   _____

Vocabulary   **6**   Eerie means
in Context   ☐ a. spooky.
       ☐ b. exciting.
       ☐ c. colorful.
       ☐ d. noisy.   _____

Add your scores for questions 1–6. Enter the total here   **Total**
and on the graph on page 215.   **Score**   _____

47 Forces and Motion

Our lives are in constant motion. We move ourselves by walking, driving, or riding. We move food and goods in trucks, ships, airplanes, and trains. We move parts and products using pulleys and conveyor belts. We move satellites into space with rockets. All the ways we move things are based on a simple <u>principle</u>. A push or a pull can make things move. A push or a pull can also change an object's direction and speed. A push or a pull is a force, and forces control the motion of objects.

Anytime you see an object move or stop moving, a force is acting on the object. For example, when you hit a hockey puck on ice, the puck speeds up. It slides across the ice for a distance. Then it slows down and stops moving. The force that causes the puck to slow down and stop is friction. Without friction, the puck would keep moving. Friction is the force between two surfaces that acts in the opposite direction of the motion. The amount of friction depends on how tightly the two surfaces are pressed together and how slick they are. Very slick surfaces, such as ice and waxed floors, create less friction than rough surfaces.

Earth's gravity affects the motion of objects too. Gravity is the force that pulls things toward the earth's surface. Consider a ball's motion when you throw it horizontally. The ball moves in the direction you threw it. The force of gravity, however, pulls down on the ball, giving it a curved path until the ball strikes the ground. Without gravity, the ball would keep moving in the direction you threw it.

We have put our understanding of forces into machines and technology. As a result, we have electrical, magnetic, aerodynamic, and other forces. These forces control motion in our homes, cities, skies, waterways, and beyond.

Main Idea	1		Answer	Score
	Mark the *main idea*		M	15
	Mark the statement that is *too broad*		B	5
	Mark the statement that is *too narrow*		N	5
	a. Gravity pulls objects toward the earth.		☐	_____
	b. Things on the earth are always moving.		☐	_____
	c. Forces control when and how objects move.		☐	_____

Subject Matter 2 The purpose of this passage is to
☐ a. explain how friction and gravity control motion.
☐ b. describe how we transport goods.
☐ c. keep people from falling on ice.
☐ d. compare pushes and pulls.   _____

Supporting Details 3 Without friction and gravity, moving objects would
☐ a. go around in circles.
☐ b. slow down and eventually stop.
☐ c. be pulled down to the earth.
☐ d. keep moving in the same direction.   _____

Conclusion 4 We can conclude from the second paragraph that
☐ a. hockey pucks slide on their own.
☐ b. an empty box could be pushed more easily across a floor than a box of books.
☐ c. there is no friction on ice.
☐ d. rough surfaces create less friction than slick surfaces do.   _____

Clarifying Devices 5 To explain gravity, the author uses the example of a
☐ a. conveyor belt.
☐ b. ball that's been thrown.
☐ c. hockey puck.
☐ d. satellite.   _____

Vocabulary in Context 6 In this passage <u>principle</u> means
☐ a. rule or law.
☐ b. head of a school.
☐ c. a belief that helps people be good.
☐ d. vision.   _____

Add your scores for questions 1–6. Enter the total here and on the graph on page 215.   **Total Score**   _____

48 A Marvel of Engineering

The Aztec Indians built their first temple on an island in 1345 A.D. The island was in the middle of swampy Lake Texcoco. A city grew up around this temple, and the Aztecs called it Tenochtitlan. The name means "Place of the Fruit of the Prickly Pear Cactus." Tenochtitlan was where Mexico City, the capital of Mexico, is today.

The Aztecs were good engineers. A 10-mile long dike held back part of the lake. It helped to control flooding. The Aztecs built three <u>causeways</u> over the swampy waters to link the city with the lakeshore. The bridges in the causeways could be removed. Then gaps were left that kept enemies from entering the city. Inside the city were canals. They linked all parts of the city. People traveling in canoes used the canals as their roads.

The engineers built stone aqueducts to bring fresh water from the mainland to the city. They also drained parts of Lake Texcoco. On the drained land, they made thousands of swamp gardens. The gardens formed a ring around the city. Ditches linked the gardens and were used to drain and irrigate the land.

Aztec houses had one story and a flat roof. In the middle of the city was a large square. In the square were the emperor's palace and the great temple. When the Spaniards arrived in 1519, about 150,000 people lived in Tenochtitlan.

The riches of the city amazed the Spaniards. They wanted Tenochtitlan for themselves. Between 1519 and 1521, Spaniards, along with native tribes, attacked the city. The Aztecs struggled to keep their city, but they were not successful. Tenochtitlan was captured in April 1521. The invaders pulled down most of the buildings. The Aztec Empire was gone forever.

Main Idea	1		Answer	Score
	Mark the *main idea*		M	15
	Mark the statement that is *too broad*		B	5
	Mark the statement that is *too narrow*		N	5

a. Remarkable engineering went into the building of Tenochtitlan ☐ _____

b. The Aztecs built a city in a lake. ☐ _____

c. The Spaniards defeated the Aztecs in 1521. ☐ _____

Score 15 points for each correct answer.   Score

Subject Matter **2** This passage is mainly about
- ☐ a. the Spanish invasion of Tenochtitlan.
- ☐ b. what Tenochtitlan looked like.
- ☐ c. Aztec gardens.
- ☐ d. important cities in Mexico.   _____

Supporting Details **3** In this passage, causeways, bridges, canals, and aqueducts are examples of
- ☐ a. Spanish engineering.
- ☐ b. Aztec wealth.
- ☐ c. Aztec religion.
- ☐ d. Aztec engineering.   _____

Conclusion **4** Tenochtitlan had canals rather than dirt roads because
- ☐ a. their engineers could not build roads.
- ☐ b. the emperor lived in the center of the city.
- ☐ c. the people were lazy.
- ☐ d. the land was swampy.   _____

Clarifying Devices **5** In the third paragraph, a clue to the meaning of *aqueduct* is
- ☐ a. the word *engineers.*
- ☐ b. the words *bring fresh water.*
- ☐ c. the words *to the city.*
- ☐ d. the word *mainland.*   _____

Vocabulary in Context **6** The word <u>causeways</u> means
- ☐ a. reasons.
- ☐ b. railways on stilts.
- ☐ c. raised roads across wet land.
- ☐ d. ferryboats.   _____

Add your scores for questions 1–6. Enter the total here and on the graph on page 215.   Total Score   _____

49 Numbers with Personality

Around 550 B.C. a Greek mathematician named Pythagoras founded a center of learning. The teachers and students who joined him were called Pythagoreans. These scholars are given <u>credit</u> for many important discoveries in mathematics. But they also spent time just playing around with number patterns. Some Pythagoreans held the belief that numbers had personality. Even numbers were feminine, while odd numbers were masculine. The number 1 represented reason, and 4 stood for justice. Some numbers were perfect; others were friendly.

These labels for numbers often depended on the number and kinds of divisors. Divisors are numbers that divide into other numbers exactly. For example, 3 is a divisor of 12 because it goes into 12 exactly 4 times. The divisors of 6 are 1, 2, 3, and the number 6 itself. The Pythagoreans called a number perfect if it equaled the sum of all the divisors except for the number itself. Since 6 equals $1 + 2 + 3$, 6 is a perfect number.

Are there a lot of perfect numbers? You might think so, but you would be wrong. The next perfect number is 28 ($1 + 2 + 4 + 7 + 14$). Then come 496, 8128, and 33,550,336. The perfect numbers are rare indeed.

Which numbers were "friendly?" Friendly numbers come in pairs. In a pair, each number is the sum of the divisors of the other. The divisors of 220 are 1, 2, 4, 5, 10, 11, 20, 22, 44, 55, and 110. Add them together and you get 284. The divisors of 284 are 1, 2, 4, 71, and 142. Their sum is 220. So 220 and 284 are friendly numbers.

Friendly numbers aren't very common either. The tenth such pair, 1184 and 1210, wasn't discovered until 1867. The discovery was made by a 16-year-old boy.

Main Idea	1	Answer	Score
	Mark the *main idea*	**M**	15
	Mark the statement that is *too broad*	**B**	5
	Mark the statement that is *too narrow*	**N**	5

a. The Pythagoreans classified numbers in several different ways. ☐ _____

b. Many numbers have interesting qualities. ☐ _____

c. There are only a few pairs of friendly numbers. ☐ _____

Subject Matter   **2**   This passage is mainly about
- ☐ a. Pythagoras.
- ☐ b. how the Pythagoreans classified numbers.
- ☐ c. what a divisor is.
- ☐ d. practical uses for perfect and friendly numbers.   _____

Supporting Details   **3**   The Pythagoreans thought that odd numbers such as 3 and 11 were
- ☐ a. perfect.
- ☐ b. friendly.
- ☐ c. feminine.
- ☐ d. masculine.   _____

Conclusion   **4**   Perfect numbers are
- ☐ a. always greater than 100.
- ☐ b. always less than one million.
- ☐ c. rare and difficult to find.
- ☐ d. common and easy to find.   _____

Clarifying Devices   **5**   The information in the last sentence is intended to
- ☐ a. surprise you.
- ☐ b. prove that math is easy.
- ☐ c. confuse you.
- ☐ d. convince you to like number patterns.   _____

Vocabulary in Context   **6**   In this passage the word <u>credit</u> means
- ☐ a. money.
- ☐ b. honor.
- ☐ c. trust.
- ☐ d. blame.   _____

Add your scores for questions 1–6. Enter the total here and on the graph on page 215.   **Total Score**   _____

50 Building with the Arch

Very early buildings were generally small and low. People did not know how to build ceilings that were high and wide. This <u>shortcoming</u> began to be overcome with the development of the arch.

An arch is a curved structure that is built over an opening. Often it is in the shape of a half circle. You have probably seen doorways with semicircular arches built above them. The important thing about arches is this: they are designed so that they do not have to be supported from the bottom. You might wonder what holds semicircular arches together. The arches are made of bricks or stones shaped like wedges. The weight of the wall above them pushes down and locks the wedges into place. If an arch is supported properly, it can span wide spaces. It does not need posts underneath to hold it up.

The ancient Romans did not develop the arch. The Egyptians did. But the Romans began to do many things with it. For example, they extended the arch into a vault, an arched ceiling or roof. At first these ceilings were just connecting series of identical arches built side by side. The semicircular buildings they covered were fairly wide. However, they were still dark. They had openings only at their ends. Then the Romans realized they could set two such buildings together at right angles. The area where they met formed a square, and this square could be given more support from underneath. It could also let in light from four different angles.

The arch was one of the most important developments in architecture. It has been used for many kinds of buildings throughout the centuries. Look at the buildings around you. You will see that it is still in use today.

Main Idea	1		
		Answer	**Score**
	Mark the *main idea*	M	15
	Mark the statement that is *too broad*	B	5
	Mark the statement that is *too narrow*	N	5

a. The arch allowed architects to build higher and wider buildings. ☐ ____

b. An arch does not have to be supported from the bottom. ☐ ____

c. There are many important developments in architecture. ☐ ____

Score 15 points for each correct answer.   **Score**

Subject Matter   **2**   The purpose of this passage is to
    ☐ a. tell about the buildings Egyptians built.
    ☐ b. show how the arch improved architecture.
    ☐ c. describe what an arch looks like.
    ☐ d. compare ancient and modern architecture.   _____

Supporting   **3**   The arch was developed by
Details
    ☐ a. the Romans.
    ☐ b. the Greeks.
    ☐ c. the Egyptians.
    ☐ d. Stone Age people.   _____

Conclusion   **4**   In order to create arches, people had to learn to
    ☐ a. build with rectangular stones.
    ☐ b. build with wedge-shaped stones.
    ☐ c. cut openings in walls for windows.
    ☐ d. work with lines and angles.   _____

Clarifying   **5**   The word *However* in paragraph 3 suggests that a
Devices
    ☐ a. contrast will follow.
    ☐ b. choice will follow.
    ☐ c. description will follow.
    ☐ d. story will follow.   _____

Vocabulary   **6**   A shortcoming is a
in Context
    ☐ a. quick trip.
    ☐ b. surprising decision.
    ☐ c. fault or defect.
    ☐ d. word of praise.   _____

Add your scores for questions 1–6. Enter the total here   **Total**
and on the graph on page 215.   **Score**   _____

51 A Balanced Diet

Your body works 24 hours a day. It's always building and repairing, feeding and cleansing itself. Its goal is to be ready for your every movement, breath, and thought. The quality of your life depends on how well your body works. And how well your body works depends on how much energy it gets. Energy comes from the food you eat. Food contains <u>nutrients</u> that your body needs for growth and energy.

By eating a balanced diet, your body gets the six essential nutrients it needs. *Minerals* are nutrients that build bones and teeth. Minerals also form red blood cells and other substances. *Water* aids digestion and waste removal. *Carbohydrates* give your body its main source of energy. Two carbohydrates are sugars from foods such as fruits and vegetables and starches found in rice, potatoes, and bread. *Fats* help build cell membranes. *Proteins* repair and grow body tissues. Finally, *vitamins* help your body use carbohydrates, fats, and proteins.

The United States Department of Agriculture (USDA) has created a nutritional food pyramid. It shows the daily number of servings you should eat from five food groups. The food pyramid has four levels. The base of the pyramid is the largest level. It contains the bread, cereal, rice, and pasta group from which you need six to eleven servings. The next level has two food groups: vegetables and fruits. The USDA recommends three to five servings of vegetables and two to four servings of fruit. The third level also has two groups: the milk, yogurt, and cheese group and the meat, poultry, fish, dry beans, eggs, and nuts group. You need two to three servings from each of these groups. The top of the pyramid is the smallest level. It contains fats, oils, and sweets. These foods have few nutrients, so eat them sparingly.

Main Idea	1	Answer	Score
	Mark the *main idea*	M	15
	Mark the statement that is *too broad*	B	5
	Mark the statement that is *too narrow*	N	5

a. Eating a balanced diet gives your body the energy it needs. ☐ _____

b. A balanced diet is important for everyone. ☐ _____

c. Meat, poultry, fish, dry beans, eggs, and nuts are on the third level. ☐ _____

Score 15 points for each correct answer.   **Score**

Subject Matter   **2**   Another good title for this passage is
- [ ] a. What You Need to Know About Fats.
- [ ] b. An Apple a Day Keeps the Doctor Away.
- [ ] c. Water: An Essential Nutrient.
- [ ] d. Eating for Life and Health.   _____

Supporting Details   **3**   A balanced diet
- [ ] a. consists of foods from five food groups.
- [ ] b. includes many foods containing fat.
- [ ] c. includes six to eleven servings of fruit.
- [ ] d. can be obtained by taking vitamins.   _____

Conclusion   **4**   The first paragraph suggests that food
- [ ] a. is something that cleanses your body.
- [ ] b. can improve the quality of your life.
- [ ] c. should be eaten at night as well as during the day.
- [ ] d. will make it easier for you to exercise.   _____

Clarifying Devices   **5**   To help the reader identify the six nutrients needed by the body, the author
- [ ] a. describes the five basic food groups.
- [ ] b. explains what a balanced diet is.
- [ ] c. writes the name of each nutrient in italics.
- [ ] d. tells the number of daily servings needed from each food group.   _____

Vocabulary in Context   **6**   A <u>nutrient</u> is
- [ ] a. a substance that gives the body energy.
- [ ] b. a type of blood cell.
- [ ] c. a body tissue.
- [ ] d. the quality of your life.   _____

Add your scores for questions 1–6. Enter the total here and on the graph on page 216.   **Total Score**   _____

52 What Did Confucius Say?

The time after 771 B.C. was a time of unrest in China. Many great thinkers wanted peace and unity. One of the greatest of these thinkers was Confucius.

Confucius lived from 551 B.C. to 479 B.C. His family was poor but of the noble class. Confucius was a good student. He studied hard. He became one of the world's most successful teachers. He had many ideas on how people should live their lives. He also had beliefs about how governments should rule. His ideas and beliefs make up a <u>code</u> of behavior. This code is called Confucianism.

Here are some of the ideas in the code. Kindness and goodness are very important. People must be sincere, loyal, and respectful. They should act this way especially with their families. Rulers must be wise and good. They should set an example. If rulers are wise and good, then their people will also be wise and good.

Confucius died at the age of 72. During his lifetime, he taught about 3,000 disciples. They believed in his ideas. They continued to teach them. One believer named Mencius spread the ideas throughout China. This happened 100 years after Confucius's death. From then on, Confucianism was popular all over the country.

During the Han dynasty, from 206 B.C. to A.D. 220, the ideas of Confucianism become a part of the way of governing. The Han dynasty combined a strong ruler with Confucian ideas. The rulers in this dynasty led their people by good example. They did not use punishment.

Main Idea 1

	Answer	Score
Mark the *main idea*	M	15
Mark the statement that is *too broad*	B	5
Mark the statement that is *too narrow*	N	5

a. Ancient China had many great thinkers. ☐ _____

b. Confucius was an important Chinese thinker. ☐ _____

c. The Han dynasty accepted the ideas of Confucianism. ☐ _____

Score 15 points for each correct answer.   **Score**

Subject Matter 　2　This passage is mainly about
- [ ] a. Confucius's life.
- [ ] b. Confucius's thinking.
- [ ] c. Chinese government.
- [ ] d. Chinese mathematics.   _____

Supporting Details 　3　Confucius taught
- [ ] a. the rulers of the Han dynasty.
- [ ] b. Mencius.
- [ ] c. about 3,000 disciples.
- [ ] d. all the great Chinese thinkers.   _____

Conclusion 　4　The Han dynasty ruled China for about
- [ ] a. 200 years.
- [ ] b. 400 years.
- [ ] c. 14 years.
- [ ] d. 1,000 years.   _____

Clarifying Devices 　5　The first paragraph of the passage
- [ ] a. compares Chinese life before and after Confucius.
- [ ] b. identifies other great Chinese thinkers.
- [ ] c. shows why the Han dynasty came to power.
- [ ] d. establishes the background for Confucius's thinking.   _____

Vocabulary in Context 　6　The word <u>code</u> in this passage means
- [ ] a. secret writing.
- [ ] b. a set of signals to send messages.
- [ ] c. rules of conduct.
- [ ] d. written laws of a nation.   _____

Add your scores for questions 1–6. Enter the total here and on the graph on page 216.   **Total Score**   _____

53 *A Raisin in the Sun*

When you turn on the TV today you see shows about black families. There are also movies and plays about African-American life. You may think that there are not enough of any of these. But there was a time when things were worse.

When *A Raisin in the Sun* opened on Broadway in 1959, it was the first time a play by an African-American woman had ever played there. Its author was Lorraine Hansberry. She would also become the first black to win the New York Drama Critics Circle Award.

Hansberry's play was based on her own life. She grew up in Chicago in a fairly well-off family. But the family had trouble when they tried to move into a white neighborhood. Segregation was common in all cities at that time. Hansberry's parents had money. They were well educated. But they were still not accepted.

In the play, Mama Younger buys a home in a white neighborhood. She uses money from her dead husband's life insurance policy. Soon after, a white man comes and offers to buy them out. He offers them "financial gain" to keep the neighborhood segregated. At first, the family angrily refuses. But later Mama's son Walter <u>reconsiders</u> the offer. His business is doing badly, and he needs the money to keep it going. Will he allow the family to be bribed like this? Or will they be able to keep their piece of the American dream?

Hansberry died of cancer at age 34. But she had written an important play. *A Raisin in the Sun* gave a realistic picture of African-American struggles. It showed how differently members of one family could look at life. It gave white audiences something to think about. And it gave hope to a whole new group of black actors and writers.

Main Idea	1	Answer	Score
	Mark the *main idea*	M	15
	Mark the statement that is *too broad*	B	5
	Mark the statement that is *too narrow*	N	5

a. *A Raisin in the Sun* is an important play about an African-American family. ☐ _____

b. *A Raisin in the Sun* was based on events in Lorraine Hansberry's own life. ☐ _____

c. There are not enough plays that focus on African-American life. ☐ _____

Score 15 points for each correct answer.   Score

Subject Matter   **2**   Another good title for this passage would be
- ☐ a. How Lorraine Hansberry Changed American Theater.
- ☐ b. The Hard Life of a Black Writer.
- ☐ c. Broadway Plays in the 1950s.
- ☐ d. Mama Younger and Her Family.   _____

Supporting Details   **3**   Hansberry's family
- ☐ a. lived in New York.
- ☐ b. sold their house to finance a family business.
- ☐ c. did not want their daughter to be a writer.
- ☐ d. were wealthy and well educated.   _____

Conclusion   **4**   Hansberry's play made black authors
- ☐ a. jealous of her success.
- ☐ b. begin to believe that there would be work for them.
- ☐ c. want to work only for black audiences.
- ☐ d. realize they could be successful while they were young.   _____

Clarifying Devices   **5**   The writer uses the phrase "piece of the American dream" to refer to a
- ☐ a. job.
- ☐ b. play.
- ☐ c. house.
- ☐ d. family.   _____

Vocabulary in Context   **6**   <u>Reconsiders</u> means
- ☐ a. refuses.
- ☐ b. answers.
- ☐ c. buys a share of.
- ☐ d. thinks about again.   _____

Add your scores for questions 1–6. Enter the total here and on the graph on page 216.   Total Score   _____

54 The "Right" Angle

What is the "right" angle? It depends, of course, on what you need the angle for. However, in mathematics, a right angle is one with a very specific size.

An angle is formed whenever two straight lines come together at a point. The size of an angle is the distance between the lines, *not* the lengths of the lines. Angles are measured in degrees using a tool called a protractor. This tool is a <u>semicircular</u> piece of plastic or metal marked in degrees. A protractor can be used to measure or to draw an angle of any desired size.

So what is a right angle? It is an angle that measures 90 degrees. One way to visualize a right angle is to think about a square or a rectangle, familiar four-sided geometric shapes. The angle in each corner of a square or rectangle is a right angle. If you cut a square in half from one corner to the opposite corner, you'll get two triangles. Each of them is a right triangle because each has one right angle. Many geometric figures have one or more right angles.

Angles that are not right angles have special names. Angles less than 90 degrees are acute angles. Angles greater than 90 degrees are obtuse angles. A triangular "Yield" sign has three acute angles. The eight-sided "Stop" sign has eight obtuse angles.

Once you start looking for right angles, you'll find them everywhere. Windows, doors, walls, and tables all make use of right angles. If the angles aren't right, the objects look crooked. If the legs of a table don't make right angles with the top, the table will wobble. In many types of construction projects, the only "right" angle is a right angle!

Main Idea   1

	Answer	Score
Mark the *main idea*	M	15
Mark the statement that is *too broad*	B	5
Mark the statement that is *too narrow*	N	5

a. A protractor is used to measure angles. ☐ _____

b. Many objects contain angles. ☐ _____

c. Right angles—angles measuring 90 degrees—are found frequently in the everyday world. ☐ _____

Subject Matter   **2**   This passage is mainly about
- ☐ a. how to measure angles.
- ☐ b. the definition of and uses for a right angle.
- ☐ c. angles measuring more than 90 degrees.
- ☐ d. squares, rectangles, and triangles.   _____

Supporting Details   **3**   An acute angle
- ☐ a. measures 90 degrees.
- ☐ b. measures more than 90 degrees.
- ☐ c. measures less than 90 degrees.
- ☐ d. is formed whenever two lines meet at a point.   _____

Conclusion   **4**   It is logical to conclude that
- ☐ a. nearly all angles are right angles.
- ☐ b. no one uses a protractor anymore.
- ☐ c. right angles are found in trees and other growing things.
- ☐ d. engineers, architects, and construction workers use right angles.   _____

Clarifying Devices   **5**   The writer helps you visualize different kinds of angles by
- ☐ a. giving examples of places they are used.
- ☐ b. describing what a table looks like.
- ☐ c. asking several questions.
- ☐ d. telling what a protractor is.   _____

Vocabulary in Context   **6**   Semicircular means shaped like
- ☐ a. an oval.
- ☐ b. a full moon.
- ☐ c. half a circle.
- ☐ d. two circles.   _____

Add your scores for questions 1–6. Enter the total here and on the graph on page 216.   **Total Score**   _____

55 Eclipses

It's a bright sunny day. Suddenly the day turns dark and stars come out. A few minutes later, bright sunlight returns. What has happened? Maybe heavenly monsters injured or killed the sun. Perhaps the sun fainted or got sick. Maybe it lost a battle with the moon. These are only some of the beliefs of ancient peoples around the world. People developed ceremonies and rituals to chase away the monsters and to honor and calm the sun and the moon. Today, most people are aware of a scientific explanation: the moon eclipsed the sun, or moved in front of it.

Eclipses occur only on rare occasions when the sun, moon, and Earth are in a straight line. A solar eclipse occurs when the moon moves between the sun and Earth. The bright sun casts the moon's shadow on part of Earth. The shadow has two parts: the umbra and the penumbra. Areas on Earth in the moon's umbra, or the shadow's center, experience a total solar eclipse. In these areas the entire sun is hidden behind the moon. In some areas the eclipse may last as long as 7.5 minutes.

Areas on Earth in the moon's penumbra, or the part of the shadow outside the umbra, experience a partial solar eclipse. In these areas only part of the sun is <u>obscured</u>. The moon's penumbra covers a larger area on Earth than the umbra does. So more areas on Earth experience partial solar eclipses than they do total solar eclipses.

A lunar eclipse occurs when Earth moves between the sun and the moon. The sun casts Earth's shadow on the moon. Similar to the moon's shadow, Earth's shadow has a central umbra surrounded by a penumbra. If the moon is in Earth's umbra, a total lunar eclipse occurs, and the whole moon darkens. If the moon is in Earth's penumbra, a partial lunar eclipse occurs. Only part of the moon darkens. People anywhere on Earth can see a lunar eclipse that occurs at normal moonlight times.

Main Idea	1		
		Answer	**Score**
Mark the *main idea*		M	15
Mark the statement that is *too broad*		B	5
Mark the statement that is *too narrow*		N	5

a. Some ancient people believed that a solar eclipse occurred when the moon destroyed the sun in battle. ☐ _____

b. Eclipses are a phenomenon of nature. ☐ _____

c. Eclipses occur when the sun casts shadows on the moon or Earth. ☐ _____

Subject Matter   **2**   Another good title for this passage is
     ☐ a. Heavenly Bodies in Battle.
     ☐ b. Beliefs and Facts About Eclipses.
     ☐ c. Totally Eclipsed Inside the Umbra.
     ☐ d. Bright Lights and Dark Shadows.   ____

Supporting   **3**   An eclipse occurs when
Details
     ☐ a. people see the moon darken.
     ☐ b. the sun gets very bright.
     ☐ c. monsters in the sky try to kill the sun or
        moon.
     ☐ d. the sun, moon, and Earth are in a line.   ____

Conclusion   **4**   We can conclude from this passage that
     ☐ a. ancient people feared eclipses.
     ☐ b. ancient people understood eclipses.
     ☐ c. many people today fear eclipses.
     ☐ d. eclipses occur about once a month.   ____

Clarifying   **5**   To show that the moon's shadow determines
Devices   whether a solar eclipse is total or partial, the author
     ☐ a. discusses the beliefs of ancient peoples.
     ☐ b. tells how long a solar eclipse may last.
     ☐ c. describes the two parts of the shadow.
     ☐ d. tells how often solar eclipses occur.   ____

Vocabulary   **6**   To be <u>obscured</u> means to be
in Context
     ☐ a. developed.
     ☐ b. hidden.
     ☐ c. viewed.
     ☐ d. moved.   ____

Add your scores for questions 1–6. Enter the total here   **Total**
and on the graph on page 216.   **Score**   ____

56 What Is Anthropology?

Ancient Greeks observed people that they conquered. Ancient Romans kept records of people on the edges of their empire. What were they doing?

Early Europeans heard about exotic people. They thought about human nature. They wondered what makes us human. They <u>pondered</u> civilization. Explorers traveled to new worlds. They came back with stories of strange people. Missionaries went to unexplored places. They wrote about the new cultures they saw.

Then scientists traveled to these new places. They wanted to study the people for themselves. They lived with the people. They observed their ways of life. Some lived with people along the Amazon. Some lived with islanders. Others lived with aborigines. They studied people's physical characteristics. They studied their customs and habits. They got ideas and formed theories. What were these scientists doing?

The scientists were doing anthropology. This is a social science that looks at human beings. It looks at differences among people. It also looks for things that humans share.

Anthropologists often look at people in groups. So in this way they are like sociologists. But generally they look at people in less developed areas of the world. They may compare life in several of these areas. Or they may compare one group with a more developed culture. They learn that some people have very unusual customs and beliefs. They learn also that some things are the same everywhere. Parents love their children. Families are important. People select leaders. It is only *how* these things are done that is different.

Main Idea　　1

	Answer	Score
Mark the *main idea*	M	15
Mark the statement that is *too broad*	B	5
Mark the statement that is *too narrow*	N	5

a.　People are interested in people.　☐　____

b.　Anthropology is the study of people.　☐　____

c.　Scientists traveled to new places to study people.　☐　____

Subject Matter   **2**   This passage is
       ☐ a. an overview of what anthropology is.
       ☐ b. a research study.
       ☐ c. a biography of an anthropologist.
       ☐ d. a personal narrative.   _____

Supporting   **3**   Some of the first people to study other cultures were
Details   ☐ a. scientists.
       ☐ b. missionaries.
       ☐ c. people along the Amazon.
       ☐ d. ancient Greeks and Romans.   _____

Conclusion   **4**   The passage suggests that
       ☐ a. some groups hate their children.
       ☐ b. certain basic values are the same in all
          societies.
       ☐ c. missionaries wanted to be conquerors.
       ☐ d. all people need to be told what to do.   _____

Clarifying   **5**   The author compares anthropology and sociology to
Devices   ☐ a. show how they are different.
       ☐ b. show why anthropology is a better area
          to study.
       ☐ c. confuse the reader.
       ☐ d. criticize certain scientists.   _____

Vocabulary   **6**   The word <u>pondered</u> means
in Context   ☐ a. carefully thought about.
       ☐ b. laughed at.
       ☐ c. explored.
       ☐ d. participated in.   _____

Add your scores for questions 1–6. Enter the total here   **Total**
and on the graph on page 216.   **Score**   _____

57 Mosques

If you travel around the world, you will see many kinds of large public buildings. Some are government buildings. Others are museums or places of worship. Some of the most distinctive large buildings are in the Middle East. They are associated with Islam, the religion of the Muslims. This religion was founded by the prophet Mohammed.

A Muslim house of worship is called a mosque. Mosques began to be built after Mohammed's death in A.D. 632. From the beginning, they were rectangular structures with open courtyards inside. They usually had one large dome over their hall of prayer. Early mosques also often had several smaller domes. All mosques are positioned so that they face the city of Mecca, the birthplace of Mohammed.

One feature that makes a mosque unique is its minarets. These are tall, thin towers. Near the top of each is a balcony. From the balcony Muslims are called to come to the mosque and pray.

The inside of mosques is usually richly decorated with artwork. Muslims do not believe this art should show people or things. So instead they use <u>intricate</u> patterns. The patterns usually involve repeated, interlocking shapes. Several colors may be used. The patterns may be painted on tiles or worked right into the plaster. The intent is to create a feeling of calm and of religious harmony.

Mosques can be found throughout the Middle East. A famous one is the Blue Mosque in Istanbul. It was built in the seventeenth century and has many domes. A strikingly modern mosque is in Kuala Lumpur in Malaysia. This mosque was built in the 1980s. Though these buildings were constructed centuries apart, both have features that make them easily recognized as mosques.

Main Idea 1		Answer	Score
Mark the *main idea*		M	15
Mark the statement that is *too broad*		B	5
Mark the statement that is *too narrow*		N	5

a. Mosques have several features that make them distinctive. ☐ _____

b. Mosques are houses of worship. ☐ _____

c. A minaret is a tower from which Muslims are called to pray. ☐ _____

Score 15 points for each correct answer.   Score

Subject Matter   **2**   This passage is mainly about
      ☐ a. Islam.
      ☐ b. the life of Mohammed.
      ☐ c. characteristics of mosques.
      ☐ d. the Blue Mosque in Istanbul.   _____

Supporting Details   **3**   A Muslim is called to prayer from the
      ☐ a. dome.
      ☐ b. courtyard.
      ☐ c. prayer hall.
      ☐ d. minaret.   _____

Conclusion   **4**   The design of mosques
      ☐ a. has not changed much over the centuries.
      ☐ b. varies according to the country a mosque is
         built in.
      ☐ c. always includes many domes.
      ☐ d. requires that they are built on hills.   _____

Clarifying Devices   **5**   The writer clarifies the meaning of *mosque* by
      ☐ a. giving an example.
      ☐ b. defining it.
      ☐ c. comparing mosques to synagogues.
      ☐ d. using a diagram.   _____

Vocabulary in Context   **6**   <u>Intricate</u> means
      ☐ a. detailed and complicated.
      ☐ b. large and clumsy.
      ☐ c. colorful.
      ☐ d. black and white.   _____

Add your scores for questions 1–6. Enter the total here   **Total**
and on the graph on page 216.   **Score**   _____

58 A Theorem Most Proved

A theorem is a math statement that has been proved true. If you have taken high school mathematics classes, you have <u>undoubtedly</u> studied or even proved theorems. The most frequently proved theorem of all time is probably one called the Pythagorean Theorem. All mathematicians know that the theorem is true. But many people, including United States President James Garfield, have entertained themselves by creating new proofs for this theorem. One book published in 1940 had more than 370 different proofs.

To understand the Pythagorean Theorem, you need to know only two things: how to square a number and the definition of a right triangle. To square a number means to multiply it by itself. The square of 3 is 3 times 3, or 9. Four squared is 16; 5 squared equals 25. A right triangle must have one right angle, an angle measuring 90 degrees. (You might remember that a right angle looks like the corner of a square.)

So, what does the Pythagorean Theorem say? It states that if you add the squares of the two short sides of a right triangle, the sum is equal to the square of the longest side. The triangle in the drawing has short sides of 3 and 4 units. Three squared is 9; four squared is 16; the sum of 9 and 16 is 25. And 25 equals the square of the long side, 5 times 5. This theorem holds true for all right triangles.

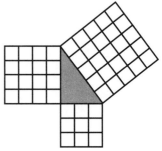

One use of this idea is in making a right angle. If you cut three pieces of wood and make them 3 feet, 4 feet, and 5 feet long, you can construct a triangle. According to the Pythagorean Theorem, this must be a right triangle. Cutting wood to these lengths is one way people create a right angle for construction or engineering projects.

Main Idea 1 ───────────────────────────────

	Answer	Score
Mark the *main idea*	M	15
Mark the statement that is *too broad*	B	5
Mark the statement that is *too narrow*	N	5

a. The Pythagorean Theorem tells how the sides of a right triangle are related. ☐ ____

b. President Garfield wrote a proof of the Pythagorean Theorem. ☐ ____

c. Many theorems in math have more than one proof. ☐ ____

Subject Matter   **2**   This passage is mainly about
☐ a. squaring numbers.
☐ b. the Pythagorean Theorem.
☐ c. triangles and their uses.
☐ d. constructing right angles from wood.   _____

Supporting Details   **3**   A right triangle has an angle of
☐ a. 30 degrees.
☐ b. 50 degrees.
☐ c. 90 degrees.
☐ d. 120 degrees.   _____

Conclusion   **4**   The diagram in the passage is intended to
☐ a. show what a square looks like.
☐ b. show that 3 plus 4 can equal 5.
☐ c. prove that not all triangles are right triangles.
☐ d. illustrate the Pythagorean Theorem.   _____

Clarifying Devices   **5**   In the last paragraph the writer describes a
☐ a. right triangle.
☐ b. proof of the Pythagorean Theorem.
☐ c. practical use of the Pythagorean Theorem.
☐ d. construction project.   _____

Vocabulary in Context   **6**   Undoubtedly means
☐ a. without a doubt.
☐ b. causing doubt.
☐ c. full of doubt.
☐ d. afraid of doubt.   _____

Add your scores for questions 1–6. Enter the total here and on the graph on page 216.   **Total Score**   _____

59 Basics of Opera

How much do you know about opera? Do you think it is just loud singing in a foreign language? If so, here is some information to give you a little background.

An opera is a musical drama. It is usually accompanied by an orchestra. Some operas are lighthearted. *The Marriage of Figaro,* with its amusing plot twists, is an example. Other operas, such as the unhappy love story of *Aida,* are serious or even tragic. The language of most operas may be foreign to you. That wasn't the writer's intention, though. Operas are sung in the language they were written in. And many composers spoke Italian or German.

Opera began in Europe in the late 1500s. Some of the earliest operas were based on Greek plays. They used a mixture of singing and reciting. Often these operas were to be performed at feasts or celebrations. The audiences were small. But opera grew quickly. Soon the performances were for large groups. The costumes were elaborate. So was the staging. There was less reciting and more singing. And not just nobles went to operas. Middle-class people went too.

Opera music is written for different kinds of voices. Here are the most common ones. A soprano is the highest female voice. It may be high and sweet or dark and dramatic. A contralto is the lowest female voice. The voice in between these is the mezzo-soprano. There are also three common male voices. The highest voice is the tenor. A little lower in range is the baritone. And lowest of all is the bass.

Operas contain arias, solo songs in which singers can show off their voices. Many arias have become popular songs all by themselves.

Main Idea	1	Answer	Score
	Mark the *main idea*	M	15
	Mark the statement that is *too broad*	B	5
	Mark the statement that is *too narrow*	N	5

a. Operas are musical dramas written for different voices.	☐	_____
b. The plots of some operas are serious.	☐	_____
c. Opera is a type of music.	☐	_____

Subject Matter   2   This passage is mostly about
- [ ] a. the first opera ever written.
- [ ] b. *The Marriage of Figaro.*
- [ ] c. the development of opera.
- [ ] d. arias.

                            _____

Supporting Details   3   The highest male voice is
- [ ] a. soprano.
- [ ] b. alto.
- [ ] c. baritone.
- [ ] d. tenor.

                            _____

Conclusion   4   We can conclude from this passage that
- [ ] a. more operas are written in Italian than in English.
- [ ] b. more arias are written for men than for women.
- [ ] c. no one writes operas today.
- [ ] d. most opera stars are German.

                            _____

Clarifying Devices   5   The ideas in the third paragraph are developed by
- [ ] a. explaining the writer's opinion.
- [ ] b. telling an interesting story.
- [ ] c. pointing out similarities and differences.
- [ ] d. creating a sad mood.

                            _____

Vocabulary in Context   6   In this passage <u>elaborate</u> means
- [ ] a. having many rich details.
- [ ] b. telling a wild story.
- [ ] c. old.
- [ ] d. sewn with silk thread.

                            _____

Add your scores for questions 1–6. Enter the total here and on the graph on page 216.   **Total Score**   _____

60 Habitat

Worms, ants, and flowers live in soil. Fish, crabs, and seaweeds live in oceans. Birds, insects, and moss live in trees. Soil, oceans, and trees are habitats—places where animals and plants live. Besides offering food and shelter, habitats allow for growth and reproduction.

Humans, however, have destroyed many habitats. We change forests into parking lots. We turn grasslands into neighborhoods. We turn beach land into resorts. We turn oceans into chemical dumps. Some plants and animals adapt and survive. Others, however, die. The changes are too much, too fast. Sometimes the death rate becomes greater than the birth rate. Then extinction occurs. An example of this happened on Florida's east coast, the habitat of the dusky seaside sparrow. This habitat changed suddenly as land was developed. And the sparrows were not able to adapt. More sparrows died than were born. In 1987 the dusky seaside sparrow became extinct. None exist in the world today.

Fortunately, <u>conservation</u> efforts are underway. Many states have set aside land for nature preserves. Here, plants and animals live in their natural habitats. Some states have created man-made habitats. Artificial reefs, for example, have been put in ocean waters. The artificial reefs are habitats for hundreds of fish and other marine life. In 1970 the federal government passed a law to protect habitats. This means that the effects of development must be studied. A highway, dam, or power plant may not be built if plants and animals are endangered. We were too late to save the dusky seaside sparrow. Hopefully, however, these new efforts will save other plants and animals.

Main Idea	1	Answer	Score
	Mark the *main idea*	M	15
	Mark the statement that is *too broad*	B	5
	Mark the statement that is *too narrow*	N	5

a. Plant and animal habitats will be destroyed unless we work to protect them. ☐ _____

b. Worms, ants, and flowers live in soil. ☐ _____

c. There are many kinds of habitats. ☐ _____

Subject Matter   **2**   This passage is concerned with
- ☐ a. federal laws.
- ☐ b. the dusky seaside sparrow.
- ☐ c. habitat protection.
- ☐ d. artificial reefs.   _____

Supporting   **3**   The worst that can happen when habitats are
Details   destroyed is that plants and animals
- ☐ a. live in their natural habitats.
- ☐ b. become extinct.
- ☐ c. adapt and survive.
- ☐ d. move to new habitats.   _____

Conclusion   **4**   The author's feeling about conservation efforts is
                           one of
- ☐ a. surprise.
- ☐ b. disrespect.
- ☐ c. hope.
- ☐ d. enthusiasm.   _____

Clarifying   **5**   The author explains the effects of habitat
Devices   destruction by presenting a
- ☐ a. real-life example.
- ☐ b. personal narrative.
- ☐ c. scientific study.
- ☐ d. made-up story.   _____

Vocabulary   **6**   In this passage <u>conservation</u> means to
in Context
- ☐ a. preserve and protect habitats.
- ☐ b. build highways, dams, and power plants.
- ☐ c. change forests into parking lots.
- ☐ d. guarantee the development of habitats.   _____

Add your scores for questions 1–6. Enter the total here   **Total**
and on the graph on page 216.   **Score**   _____

61 What Do the Fossils Tell Us?

One special branch of anthropology is archaeology. Archaeologists are scientists who look at fossil bones and tools. They look at other artifacts from long ago too. They use the fossils to put together a picture of early people. They can tell who people were. They can tell how people lived. Three-million-year-old bones can tell how ancient humans walked. Stone tools help tell what things they made and how they made them. Campfire ashes hold clues to what people ate.

One special discovery was the Neanderthal fossils. The fossils were found in 1856 in the Neander Valley, near Dusseldorf, Germany, by quarrymen. Much fossil information was lost when the site was blasted for its rocks, but something interesting was discovered. Scientists found evidence that these <u>prehistoric</u> people may have cared about each other.

At first scientists thought the fossil evidence showed that Neanderthals stooped over. They thought that they walked with their knees bent. More study showed that Neanderthals actually had arthritis. Arthritis is a crippling disease that caused the older people to bend over. These fossils provide evidence that the Neanderthal people took care of one another. Life millions of years ago was very harsh. Without care, a handicapped person would not have lived to an old age.

The graves had more evidence of caring. One man was buried on a bed of wildflowers. A teenage boy was buried with an ax and food. Perhaps the wildflowers show that someone was sad at the young man's death. Perhaps the ax and food were things it was thought the boy needed for his life after death. Perhaps the Neanderthals were not as limited as scientists first thought.

Main Idea	1	Answer	Score
	Mark the *main idea*	M	15
	Mark the statement that is *too broad*	B	5
	Mark the statement that is *too narrow*	N	5

a. Wildflowers were found in Neanderthal graves. ☐ _____

b. Fossils give evidence of how Neanderthals lived. ☐ _____

c. Archaeologists are scientists. ☐ _____

Subject Matter   **2**   This passage is mainly about
☐ a. people caring for each other.
☐ b. bones found in a quarry.
☐ c. what fossils reveal about Neanderthals.
☐ d. fossils.   _____

Supporting   **3**   Arthritis caused Neanderthals to
Details   ☐ a. live to a very old age.
☐ b. be crippled and bent over.
☐ c. die.
☐ d. be buried with wildflowers.   _____

Conclusion   **4**   The final paragraph suggests that
☐ a. very few prehistoric peoples cared for each
other.
☐ b. most Neanderthals died young.
☐ c. wildflowers grew everywhere during the
Neanderthal era.
☐ d. archaeologists are not always right.   _____

Clarifying   **5**   The first paragraph of this passage
Devices   ☐ a. introduces the Neanderthal people.
☐ b. asks a question that will be answered in
the passage.
☐ c. tells what archaeologists think about
prehistoric life.
☐ d. defines the job of an archaeologist.   _____

Vocabulary   **6**   Prehistoric means
in Context   ☐ a. the time before written history.
☐ b. gentle.
☐ c. anxious and tense.
☐ d. from a historical and important time.   _____

Add your scores for questions 1–6. Enter the total here   **Total**
and on the graph on page 216.   **Score**   _____

62 Distances and Light Years

You've probably measured length with a ruler. You may have used inches as the unit of measurement, or you may have used centimeters. There are many different units used to measure length. In addition to inches and centimeters, there are feet, yards, miles, and kilometers.

But how are *really* long distances measured? For example, the average distance from Earth to the sun is about 93 million miles. Distances like this one are not measured, of course. No one takes a long tape measure and stretches it from Earth to the sun! These types of distances are computed using other mathematical quantities.

Distances outside our solar system can be really huge. The nearest star, Proxima Centauri, is 25 trillion miles away. Written out, this distance is 25,000,000,000,000 miles. These very large numbers become difficult to write and use. So, in the late 1880s, scientists invented a very large unit of measure. They called it the light year. This is the distance that light travels in one solar year, 365 days.

Light travels very quickly indeed. The speed of light is about 186,000 miles per second. Light from the moon gets to us in 1.25 seconds, whereas light from the sun takes about 8.25 minutes. Even from Pluto, the most distant planet in our solar system, it takes about 6 hours for light to travel the distance to Earth. In 365 days, light travels about 5.9 trillion miles. So a light year was defined to be that distance. The term *light year* is a little misleading because a light year is a measure of distance, not time.

In light years, the distance from us to Proxima Centauri is 4.2. The brightest star, Sirius, is 8.7 light years distant. Light years turn <u>astronomical</u> distances into smaller numbers. These numbers are easier to use and remember.

Main Idea	1		
		Answer	**Score**
	Mark the *main idea*	M	15
	Mark the statement that is *too broad*	B	5
	Mark the statement that is *too narrow*	N	5
	a. It is 25 trillion miles to the nearest star.	☐	_____
	b. It can be interesting to study facts about stars and planets.	☐	_____
	c. Light years are used to measure very long distances.	☐	_____

Score 15 points for each correct answer.   Score

Subject Matter   2   This passage is mainly about
☐ a. measuring distances to stars.
☐ b. the solar system.
☐ c. different types of stars.
☐ d. the distance from Earth to the sun.   _____

Supporting   3   A light year is a distance equal to about
Details
☐ a. 93 million miles.
☐ b. 25 trillion miles.
☐ c. 365 days.
☐ d. 5.9 trillion miles.   _____

Conclusion   4   The distance from Earth to the moon is usually
not described in light years because this distance
☐ a. is too long.
☐ b. is too short.
☐ c. changes at different times of the year.
☐ d. has not yet been measured accurately.   _____

Clarifying   5   In the first paragraph, the writer
Devices
☐ a. explains how to use a ruler.
☐ b. mentions familiar units of measurement.
☐ c. describes different stars in the night sky.
☐ d. defines the speed of light.   _____

Vocabulary   6   In this passage the word <u>astronomical</u> means
in Context
☐ a. scientific.
☐ b. amazing.
☐ c. having to do with stars and planets.
☐ d. having to do with measuring.   _____

Add your scores for questions 1–6. Enter the total here   Total
and on the graph on page 216.   Score   _____

125

63 Impressionism

Do you ever visit art museums? If you do, you probably know which kinds of paintings are most popular. Museum directors are smart. They want to draw big crowds. One way to attract people is to have shows featuring artists such as Renoir, Monet, or Cezanne. These painters, together with several others, are called Impressionists. Modern audiences seem to love their work.

They were not always so popular, however. When their work was first shown, people laughed at it. (This was from the late 1860s into the 1880s.) Critics called their paintings half-finished. They found the colors strange and unreal. The painters were accused of "fragmenting reality"—of breaking it into pieces.

There was a reason for all the complaints. Before the Impressionists, paintings were strictly realistic. But these artists wanted to do something different. They wanted to capture what something looked like at a particular moment. And to do this, they had to work quickly. That is why some critics thought their work looked unfinished. The painters were, in fact, trying to <u>convey</u> an impression.

Impressionists were especially interested in how light affected a scene. Perhaps you have seen some of Monet's paintings of haystacks. In each painting the colors change slightly. That is because each one was painted at a slightly different time of day.

Most Impressionist painters loved the outdoors. Renoir, for example, often painted pictures of people. Many of these paintings were set in parks, gardens, or outdoor cafes. Many show the sunlight gleaming on the people's faces and bodies.

Most Impressionist art is lively and beautiful. People like its lovely colors and soft effects. But Impressionism is important beyond that. For the first time artists tried to look at familiar things in new ways.

Main Idea	1		Answer	Score
	Mark the *main idea*		M	15
	Mark the statement that is *too broad*		B	5
	Mark the statement that is *too narrow*		N	5

a.	Impressionist paintings try to capture the light at a specific moment in time.	☐	____
b.	Impressionism was an important movement in painting.	☐	____
c.	Renoir often used parks as a setting.	☐	

Score 15 points for each correct answer.   **Score**

Subject Matter   **2**   This passage is mainly about
☐ a. characteristics of Impressionist paintings.
☐ b. famous Impressionist painters.
☐ c. a history of nineteenth century art.
☐ d. why Impressionist paintings were colorful.   _____

Supporting Details   **3**   Impressionist painters
☐ a. tried to be very realistic.
☐ b. were immediately successful.
☐ c. often painted outdoors.
☐ d. took a lot of time to create their paintings.   _____

Conclusion   **4**   Based on early reactions to the Impressionists, you can conclude that people
☐ a. quickly appreciate new painting styles.
☐ b. often reject new painting styles.
☐ c. rarely like paintings of the outdoors.
☐ d. don't like paintings with too much color.   _____

Clarifying Devices   **5**   The writer talks about Renoir and Monet
☐ a. to show how different they were.
☐ b. to name some of their most famous works.
☐ c. to help explain some of the characteristics of Impressionism.
☐ d. because their work is hard to understand.   _____

Vocabulary in Context   **6**   In this passage <u>convey</u> means
☐ a. carry from one place to another.
☐ b. communicate.
☐ c. destroy.
☐ d. tell lies about.   _____

Add your scores for questions 1–6. Enter the total here and on the graph on page 216.   **Total Score**   _____

127

64 DNA Identification

Have you noticed recent news headlines like these? "Inmates Freed After DNA Tests Prove Innocence." "Thomas Jefferson DNA Study Causes an American Controversy." "DNA Tests Confirm Babies Were Swapped."

Where is your DNA? Sneeze into a tissue—your DNA is on the tissue. Lick an envelope—your DNA is on the seal. In fact, DNA is in almost every cell of your body.

What is DNA? It is a substance found in the chromosomes of cells. A chromosome is a chain of genes. Each gene carries a piece of information for a trait such as eye color, hair texture, or nose shape. More than one gene is needed for a trait to be expressed. For example, one gene will contain information for skin color. But up to six genes that carry skin color information will produce the color of your skin. Other genes carry a piece of information for other traits. Traits from grandparents, great-grandparents, and so on are passed to you through your parents. All the traits arrange themselves in patterns that are unique. No one, except an identical twin, has the same patterns that you have. DNA acts like a file that stores your unique patterns of traits.

How is DNA used in identification? DNA is obtained from a sample of blood, skin cells, hair, or saliva. The DNA is treated with a chemical, which breaks the DNA into parts. Each part contains one or more patterns of traits. Next, each part of DNA is copied many hundreds of times. Then the parts are put on a gel-like substance, and an electrical current is run through them. The current moves the pieces through the gel, leaving a trail of black bars—like bar codes. Scientists call these bars "DNA fingerprints"; and just like real fingerprints, these DNA prints are distinct for every person (except an identical twin). Scientists use the DNA identification process to <u>confirm</u> the identity of people both living and dead.

Main Idea	1		
		Answer	**Score**
	Mark the *main idea*	M	15
	Mark the statement that is *too broad*	B	5
	Mark the statement that is *too narrow*	N	5
	a. DNA is found in cells.	☐	_____
	b. No one besides an identical twin has the same DNA as you do.	☐	_____
	c. DNA provides information about traits that is being used to identify people.	☐	_____

Score 15 points for each correct answer.　　　**Score**

Subject Matter　**2**　This passage is mainly about
- ☐ a. where DNA is found.
- ☐ b. how DNA is used to identify people.
- ☐ c. DNA and identical twins.
- ☐ d. DNA stories in the news.　　　　＿＿＿

Supporting Details　**3**　DNA stores each person's
- ☐ a. patterns of traits.
- ☐ b. fingerprints.
- ☐ c. bar codes.
- ☐ d. body cells.　　　　＿＿＿

Conclusion　**4**　From information in the passage, you can conclude that which of the following is **not** a human trait?
- ☐ a. having blond hair
- ☐ b. having freckles
- ☐ c. being late often
- ☐ d. having dimples　　　　＿＿＿

Clarifying Devices　**5**　The phrase "DNA fingerprint" suggests that DNA
- ☐ a. is shaped like a person's thumb.
- ☐ b. is identified by its swirls.
- ☐ c. has tiny fingers that push it through a cell.
- ☐ d. is as unique as a person's fingerprint.　　　　＿＿＿

Vocabulary in Context　**6**　In this passage <u>confirm</u> means
- ☐ a. strengthen a person's beliefs.
- ☐ b. deny.
- ☐ c. test.
- ☐ d. prove the accuracy of.　　　　＿＿＿

Add your scores for questions 1–6. Enter the total here and on the graph on page 216.　　　**Total Score**　＿＿＿

65 Renaissance: A Rebirth of Thinking

The word *Renaissance* (REN uh sahns) comes from a French word meaning "rebirth." It is the time in Europe from the 1300s to the late 1500s. This was a time of the rebirth of ancient Roman ideas. It was also a time of new ideas.

The invention of the printing press was crucial in spreading Renaissance ideas. The new movable type press was first used in Europe in 1455. Before then most books had been copied by hand. Some were printed from carved wooden blocks. The new press made it possible to print books quickly and cheaply. Books and pamphlets became more available to everyone. More people knew how to read than ever before.

Renaissance people began to think learning was important. Wealthy people and artists explored new ideas. Scientists studied medicine and physics. They studied mathematics. They made new discoveries. <u>Humanists</u> had ideas on how to solve society's problems. They had ideas of how to care for fellow human beings.

The Renaissance had another side too. Some people studied magic and astrology. Some people were punished for being witches. Some said society was evil and corrupt. Others wanted governments to be more fair. Others protested the church. They said its leaders were concerned more with money and power than with religion. This was the dark side of the Renaissance.

The end of the Renaissance did not come at any one point. It ended at different times in different countries. It ended when political and church leaders no longer supported the new ideas. It ended when those in power feared that new learning would lead to dangerous thinking.

Main Idea   1

	Answer	Score
Mark the *main idea*	M	15
Mark the statement that is *too broad*	B	5
Mark the statement that is *too narrow*	N	5

a. Renaissance scientists made new discoveries. ☐ ____

b. The Renaissance was a period of new thinking and ideas. ☐ ____

c. The Renaissance was a period in Europe. ☐ ____

Score 15 points for each correct answer.   Score

Subject Matter **2** Another good title for this passage would be
- ☐ a. The Importance of Making Books.
- ☐ b. A Period More Evil than Good.
- ☐ c. Many Scientists and Artists.
- ☐ d. A Time of New Ideas.   _____

Supporting Details **3** What Renaissance invention made it possible to quickly print books?
- ☐ a. the wheel
- ☐ b. the printing press
- ☐ c. paper
- ☐ d. written language   _____

Conclusion **4** What led to the end of the Renaissance?
- ☐ a. printing presses no longer being used
- ☐ b. the acceptance of magic and witches
- ☐ c. the beginning of the sixteenth century
- ☐ d. a fear of new ideas   _____

Clarifying Devices **5** The writer explains the meaning of *Renaissance* through
- ☐ a. personal narrative.
- ☐ b. an explanation of the printing press.
- ☐ c. definition and examples.
- ☐ d. question and answer.   _____

Vocabulary in Context **6** In this passage the word <u>humanists</u> means
- ☐ a. people concerned with the study of human interests.
- ☐ b. people who read books and pamphlets.
- ☐ c. people who sing with closed lips.
- ☐ d. all leaders of the church.   _____

Add your scores for questions 1–6. Enter the total here and on the graph on page 216.   Total Score   _____

131

66 Slicing a Cone

Imagine an upside-down cone, like an ice cream cone. Now imagine that the cone is made of a soft material like clay. If you slice through the cone parallel to its base, the cross section you get will be a circle. A circle is one of a group of curves called *conic sections.*

You can get two more conic sections by slicing the cone at different angles. If you try to get a circle but don't cut the cone exactly parallel to the base, you'll get an oval cross section. This figure is called an *ellipse.* Hold the knife above the cone and slice down through one side. The cut will make a curve called a *parabola.*

The fourth conic section is a *hyperbola.* To get a hyperbola, you need two cones. Put them point to point. Now slice down straight through them. The cross sections that you get look somewhat like parentheses back-to-back:) (. These two cross sections together are a hyperbola.

Circles, ellipses, parabolas, and hyperbolas are important mathematical shapes. Circles are needed to create cylinder-shaped tanks of different sizes and volumes. The path of a baseball is a parabola. So are the shapes of telescopic mirrors, automobile headlights, and radar antennas. The orbits of the planets in our solar system are ellipses. LORAN, a system of <u>navigation</u>, is based on hyperbolas. It aids ships or planes in determining their positions.

Main Idea	1		
		Answer	**Score**
	Mark the *main idea*	M	15
	Mark the statement that is *too broad*	B	5
	Mark the statement that is *too narrow*	N	5

a. The path of Earth around the sun is an ellipse. ☐ ____

b. Mathematics uses many different shapes and figures. ☐ ____

c. Four conic sections are the result of slicing through a cone or a double cone. ☐ ____

Score 15 points for each correct answer.   Score

Subject Matter 2 This passage is mostly concerned with
- ☐ a. what a cone looks like.
- ☐ b. different kinds of conic sections.
- ☐ c. the difference between circles and ellipses.
- ☐ d. the paths of moving objects.   _____

Supporting Details 3 Slicing a cone parallel to its base will create
- ☐ a. an ellipse.
- ☐ b. a parabola.
- ☐ c. a hyperbola.
- ☐ d. a circle.   _____

Conclusion 4 It seems logical to conclude that conic sections
- ☐ a. have many applications in the real world.
- ☐ b. are used mainly to draw designs.
- ☐ c. are of interest only to mathematicians.
- ☐ d. only make sense in diagrams.   _____

Clarifying Devices 5 The diagram in the article shows all the conic sections **except**
- ☐ a. a circle.
- ☐ b. an ellipse.
- ☐ c. a hyperbola.
- ☐ d. a parabola.   _____

Vocabulary in Context 6 <u>Navigation</u> means the art of
- ☐ a. traveling by boat.
- ☐ b. figuring out a ship's position or course.
- ☐ c. drawing cones.
- ☐ d. proving the statements a person makes.   _____

Add your scores for questions 1–6. Enter the total here and on the graph on page 216.   Total Score   _____

67 Latin Dances

Are you part of the Latin dance craze? Do you love to samba? Maybe you can even do the tango. Did you ever stop to wonder how these and other Latin dances developed? Some have a very interesting history.

The samba is a Brazilian dance. Its origins go back to the African slaves who were brought to Brazil in the 1500s. In one of their dances a couple danced in the center of a circle. Those forming the circle performed steps similar to those of the Charleston. They also clapped and beat on drums. Later, the African dances combined with swaying steps of the dances of Indians who lived in the region. And finally, the dance became part of "polite society." It was toned down a little, but kept the hip movements it always had. Today, the samba uses many kinds of steps.

The merengue is a dance from the Dominican Republic. It may be danced to a variety of tempos, and it uses a foot-dragging step. There are two stories about this step. One is that it came from slaves who were chained together. The chains forced them to drag one leg while they worked to the beat of drums in the sugar fields. The other story is about a war hero. This man, whom some identify as General Merengie, returned home with a leg injury. People showed their sympathy for him by dragging one foot as they danced.

The tango originated in Argentina. In the late 1800s many immigrants poured into the slums of Buenos Aires, the capital city. Some spent time in bars and dance halls. There the tango developed. It used a combination of African, Indian, and European influences. It expressed people's sorrow and frustrations. The very earliest versions were considered indecent. Later, the tango was <u>sanitized</u> a bit. Then it became a dance of mainstream society.

Main Idea   **1**

	Answer	Score
Mark the *main idea*	M	15
Mark the statement that is *too broad*	B	5
Mark the statement that is *too narrow*	N	5

a. There are a lot of popular Latin dances. ☐ _____

b. Three Latin dances have interesting histories. ☐ _____

c. African slaves began the development of the samba. ☐ _____

Subject Matter   **2**   This passage is mainly about
- [ ] a. the history of the tango.
- [ ] b. how three Latin dances developed.
- [ ] c. the steps in three Latin dances.
- [ ] d. why there is a Latin dance craze.

_____

Supporting Details   **3**   The merengue comes from
- [ ] a. Argentina.
- [ ] b. Brazil.
- [ ] c. Puerto Rico.
- [ ] d. the Dominican Republic.

_____

Conclusion   **4**   We can conclude from this passage that many Latin dances were
- [ ] a. a lot wilder when they were first developed than they are now.
- [ ] b. first danced by the rich people in society.
- [ ] c. brought to Latin America from Europe.
- [ ] d. brought to the United States fairly recently.

_____

Clarifying Devices   **5**   When the author says immigrants "poured into the slums," the meaning is that they
- [ ] a. drank a lot.
- [ ] b. came in great numbers.
- [ ] c. put up with constant rainstorms.
- [ ] d. danced in the slums.

_____

Vocabulary in Context   **6**   In this passage <u>sanitized</u> means
- [ ] a. washed.
- [ ] b. hung out to dry.
- [ ] c. cleaned up.
- [ ] d. made easier to dance.

_____

Add your scores for questions 1–6. Enter the total here and on the graph on page 216.   **Total Score**   _____

135

68 Asteroids

Maybe Chicken Little knew about asteroids when he cried, "The sky is falling!" Asteroids are bits of metallic rock that were left over when our solar system was formed. Asteroids vary in size: some are only a few feet wide while others are several hundred miles across. Most asteroids orbit the Sun in a donut-shaped path between Mars and Jupiter. Some asteroids, though, cross the paths of planets. If these asteroids get pushed from their normal orbits, then they may end up in a collision course with a planet. Many asteroids have struck Earth and the moon in the past. Some scientists think that an asteroid six miles wide struck Earth 65 million years ago. The <u>impact</u> might have killed the dinosaurs and other forms of life on Earth.

Astronomers recently discovered asteroid 1997 XF11. The asteroid is one mile wide and traveling at a speed of 45,000 miles per hour. Some astronomers think 1997 XF11 is on a collision course with Earth. Others think the chance of a direct hit is zero. Calculations put the asteroid between 54,000 and 600,000 miles from Earth in the year 2028. If 1997 XF11 hits Earth, it could destroy life on all parts of our planet. Some effects would be tidal waves, fires across whole continents, and a giant dust cloud that would cool the atmosphere and disrupt agriculture.

Astronomers know that Earth will be hit by an asteroid in the future. They have different ideas about how to head off an asteroid impact. One idea is to give each asteroid an "impact risk" number. The higher the number, the greater the chance that the asteroid would hit Earth. If the impact risk is great, then more steps would be taken. Explosives could be put on or near the asteroid. The force of the explosion would push the asteroid away from Earth

Main Idea   1

	Answer	Score
Mark the *main idea*	M	15
Mark the statement that is *too broad*	B	5
Mark the statement that is *too narrow*	N	5

a. Many objects exist and orbit in space. ☐ _____

b. Asteroids can cause great damage if they collide with Earth. ☐ _____

c. Asteroid 1997 XF11 is one mile wide. ☐ _____

Score 15 points for each correct answer.   **Score**

Subject Matter 2 This passage is mainly about
☐ a. asteroids striking Earth.
☐ b. 1997 XF11.
☐ c. how astronomers discover asteroids.
☐ d. how scientists think dinosaurs died.   _____

Supporting Details 3 Most asteroids are
☐ a. in an orbit around Earth.
☐ b. only a few feet wide.
☐ c. between Mars and Jupiter.
☐ d. on a collision course with Earth.   _____

Conclusion 4 An "impact risk" number most resembles a number used
☐ a. for a date, like 6/14/01.
☐ b. to show time, like 1:15 P.M.
☐ c. to show distance, like 4,000 miles.
☐ d. to show the strength of an earthquake, like 7.2.   _____

Clarifying Devices 5 The author begins the passage with a mention of Chicken Little to
☐ a. show that children's stories are usually true.
☐ b. get you interested.
☐ c. give a clue that the passage will be funny.
☐ d. frighten you.   _____

Vocabulary in Context 6 In this passage <u>impact</u> means
☐ a. death.
☐ b. crash or collision.
☐ c. type of metallic rock.
☐ d. orbit.   _____

Add your scores for questions 1–6. Enter the total here and on the graph on page 216.   **Total Score**   _____

69 What Is Political Science?

Political science is the study of power. It looks at how governments use power. It looks at how individuals use power. It looks at how groups control each other.

Political scientists want to know how nations are governed. They want to know how social groups are organized. They ask, "How do institutions work?"

One tool political scientists use is public opinion polls. Political scientists look at how voters influence public policy. They ask, "Which groups influence elections?" They look at the demands of interest groups. They ask, "How do groups influence laws?" Political scientists also look at the impact of <u>mass media</u>. They want to know what role the media play. They ask, "How do TV, radio, newspapers, and books change people's views?"

Political scientists want to know about nations. They ask questions like the following. How do nations cooperate? What are the ties between them? How do conflicts emerge? How are conflicts resolved? Political scientists also compare political systems. They try to find out who depends on whom. They study international legal systems. They study agreements between nations.

During the 1960s, political science changed. The 1960s were a time of disagreement. Before then much of political science was theory. But during that time, many political scientists turned to issues. Scholars wanted to deal with values and facts. They got involved with the Vietnam War. They looked at causes for inner city riots. They examined the impact of assassinations.

Today theory blends with values. Topics such as peace, justice, and human rights are discussed. These values are now part of the study of political science.

Main Idea   1

	Answer	Score
Mark the *main idea*	M	15
Mark the statement that is *too broad*	B	5
Mark the statement that is *too narrow*	N	5

a. Political science is a course of study.	☐	_____
b. Political science is the study of how governments and groups use power.	☐	_____
c. Political science began examining issues in the 1960s.	☐	_____

Subject Matter   **2**   Another good title for this passage is

     ☐ a. How to Become a Political Scientist.

     ☐ b. What Political Scientists Want to Know.

     ☐ c. Political Science in the 1960s.

     ☐ d. Political Science and Television.   _____

Supporting   **3**   Public opinion polls help political scientists
Details   understand

     ☐ a. how people fill out surveys.

     ☐ b. how voters influence public policy.

     ☐ c. international legal systems.

     ☐ d. how peace can be achieved.   _____

Conclusion   **4**   What conclusion can the reader draw from the
                    many questions asked in this passage?

     ☐ a. Very little is known about political science.

     ☐ b. Political scientists ask many questions in
         their search for knowledge.

     ☐ c. Political scientists have all the answers.

     ☐ d. The reader should know the answers to
         these questions.   _____

Clarifying   **5**   In the repeated phrase "They ask" in this passage,
Devices   *They* refers to

     ☐ a. governments.

     ☐ b. voters.

     ☐ c. political scientists.

     ☐ d. public opinion polls.   _____

Vocabulary   **6**   The term <u>mass media</u> means
in Context

     ☐ a. interest groups.

     ☐ b. voters.

     ☐ c. personal letters, diaries, journals.

     ☐ d. TV, radio, newspapers, books.   _____

Add your scores for questions 1–6. Enter the total here   **Total**
and on the graph on page 216.   **Score**   _____

70 Sherlock Holmes Solves a Math Problem

Doing mathematics is much like solving a mystery. If a math problem is challenging, you may look for clues, try different approaches, or start by gathering data. Above all, you need logical reasoning.

One of the most famous logical reasoners of all is the fictional character Sherlock Holmes. In the stories and novels of Arthur Conan Doyle, Holmes and his loyal friend Watson solve a wide variety of mysteries. Holmes considers detection a science. When Watson reports their adventures, Holmes can be impatient if Watson emphasizes the exciting drama more than the pure logic.

"The Adventure of the Musgrave Ritual" is a typical Sherlock Holmes story. In the story, facts seem to lead to a hidden treasure. Holmes realizes that he needs to find the end of the shadow of an elm tree at a certain time. However, the elm has been cut down. Another character remembers that the elm was 64 feet tall. So Holmes uses a six-foot fishing pole and a little math. The six-foot pole casts a shadow nine feet long. Holmes draws a diagram like the one at the right, showing the pole and its shadow. Holmes knows that the shadow of the

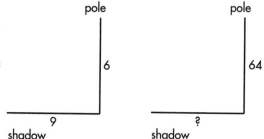

tree will be <u>proportionally</u> as long as the shadow of the pole. Doing a little math, he figures that the shadow of the 64-foot tree was 96 feet long.

The next time you have a difficult math problem to do, remember Sherlock Holmes. He found his math skills useful in his work. Someday you may too.

Main Idea   1 ——————————————————————————————

	Answer	Score
Mark the *main idea*	M	15
Mark the statement that is *too broad*	B	5
Mark the statement that is *too narrow*	N	5

a. Sherlock Holmes once used mathematics to solve a mystery. ☐ ____

b. Math has many uses in real life. ☐ ____

c. Holmes needed to find the length of the elm tree's shadow. ☐ ____

140

Subject Matter   2   Another good title for this passage would be
☐ a. Drawing a Picture.
☐ b. How Long Was the Shadow?
☐ c. Solving Mysteries.
☐ d. Measuring a Fishing Pole.   _____

Supporting Details   3   In the math problem described in the passage, Sherlock Holmes wants to find the
☐ a. time at which an elm tree was cut down.
☐ b. length of the shadow of a 6-foot pole.
☐ c. height of an elm that is no longer there.
☐ d. length of the shadow of an elm that is no longer there.   _____

Conclusion   4   The missing number in the diagram should be
☐ a. 6
☐ b. 9.
☐ c. 64.
☐ d. 96.   _____

Clarifying Devices   5   The writer points out an everyday use of math by
☐ a. giving facts about shadows.
☐ b. telling about Arthur Conan Doyle's life.
☐ c. explaining how to solve a murder mystery.
☐ d. telling a story.   _____

Vocabulary in Context   6   In this passage the word <u>proportionally</u> has to do with
☐ a. one object in relation to another.
☐ b. opposites.
☐ c. lengths.
☐ d. surprises.   _____

Add your scores for questions 1–6. Enter the total here and on the graph on page 216.

Total Score   _____

71 Epic Poems

Some of the very earliest poems were not written down. These poems were not lyrics describing scenes or emotions. Instead, they were long narratives about warfare and courage. They told stories of daring deeds and heroes. These poems are known as epics.

The tellers of epics wanted their listeners to hear exciting tales. But they also wanted them to appreciate the bravery of their ancestors. Many epics have to do with the early history of a people. One epic, Virgil's *Aeneid* (ah NEE id), for example, tells the story of the founding of Rome.

Epics are usually built around the adventures of a hero. This individual often saves his people from monsters or gods who hate them. He may travel great distances or fight in terrible battles. People would learn about how brave the hero was. So they would develop pride in their tribe or nationality. They would also learn a code of conduct. They learned how people in their tribe were expected to act.

Usually there is some <u>kernel</u> of truth in a tale of an epic hero. But there is also a lot of exaggeration. These stories were told and retold. As time passed, the heroes got braver and did more.

There are many famous epic poems. Two by the Greek poet Homer are the *Iliad* (IL ee ad) and the *Odyssey*. The *Iliad* is a story of the Trojan war. In it the Greek hero Achilles helps to defeat the Trojans. The *Odyssey* recounts Odysseus's adventures as he tried for 20 years to sail back home from the Trojan War. *Beowulf* relates the story of how the early English hero Beowulf killed a monster. *El Cid* is about the battles of the national hero of Spain.

Main Idea	1		
		Answer	**Score**
Mark the *main idea*		M	15
Mark the statement that is *too broad*		B	5
Mark the statement that is *too narrow*		N	5

a. The *Iliad* and the *Odyssey* are well-known epics. ☐ _____

b. Epics are lengthy narratives about the daring deeds of heroes. ☐ _____

c. Epics are long poems. ☐ _____

Score 15 points for each correct answer.   **Score**

Subject Matter **2** This passage mostly presents
- [ ] a. characteristics and examples of epics.
- [ ] b. the history of epics.
- [ ] c. the *Iliad* and the *Odyssey*.
- [ ] d. several famous epic heroes.

_____

Supporting Details **3** The stories in epics
- [ ] a. were completely true.
- [ ] b. were completely false.
- [ ] c. contained some truth, but also exaggeration.
- [ ] d. were often hard to understand.

_____

Conclusion **4** Epics helped people
- [ ] a. learn how to read.
- [ ] b. realize that they were better than other tribes.
- [ ] c. learn about how their gods could betray them.
- [ ] d. develop closer ties with their ancestors.

_____

Clarifying Devices **5** The final paragraph of this passage is developed through
- [ ] a. stories about Homer.
- [ ] b. examples.
- [ ] c. comparison and contrast.
- [ ] d. vivid descriptions of settings.

_____

Vocabulary in Context **6** In this passage <u>kernel</u> means a
- [ ] a. piece of corn.
- [ ] b. small amount.
- [ ] c. military leader.
- [ ] d. traveler.

_____

Add your scores for questions 1–6. Enter the total here and on the graph on page 216.

Total Score _____

72 The Scientific Method

Did you ever wonder why the water level in a glass doesn't change when the ice in the glass melts? To find out why, you can use the scientific method. Used by scientists in various situations, the scientific method is also a clear and logical way to solve many real-world problems, as the procedure below indicates.

Steps in the Scientific Method	Example
State the problem or question.	"Why doesn't the water level in a glass rise when ice melts?"
Using your own observations and research, <u>compile</u> information about the problem.	You already know that ice is frozen water. From your research, you learn that water and ice are made of water molecules.
Form a hypothesis, or a best guess based on the information.	"The molecules in water appear to be closer together than they are in ice."
Test the hypothesis by doing an experiment.	Fill four glasses with ice. Then pour water over the ice and fill each glass to the rim. As the ice melts, you observe that the water does not spill over the top of the glasses. Each time you repeat the experiment, you get the same results.
Draw a conclusion based on your results.	Molecules are closer together in water than they are in ice.

Main Idea 1 _____

	Answer	Score
Mark the *main idea*	M	15
Mark the statement that is *too broad*	B	5
Mark the statement that is *too narrow*	N	5

a. Scientists like to figure out problems. ☐ _____

b. One step in the scientific method is to test the hypothesis. ☐ _____

c. The steps in the scientific method help people solve problems. ☐ _____

Score 15 points for each correct answer. Score

Subject Matter **2** Another good title for this passage would be
☐ a. Are You Curious?
☐ b. Water and Ice Don't Mix.
☐ c. Follow the Steps to Find Out Why.
☐ d. Hypothesis and Conclusion. _____

Supporting Details **3** A hypothesis is
☐ a. a guess about the cause of something.
☐ b. a conclusion about water molecules.
☐ c. the first step in the scientific method.
☐ d. an experiment. _____

Conclusion **4** This passage suggests that
☐ a. doing an experiment will always prove that your hypothesis is correct.
☐ b. the scientific method is a logical way to solve problems.
☐ c. research should be done only in books.
☐ d. few scientists use the scientific method anymore. _____

Clarifying Devices **5** The chart structure in the passage is useful because it
☐ a. compares and contrasts water and ice.
☐ b. shows a diagram of how ice melts.
☐ c. explains cause and effect.
☐ d. clearly shows steps and examples. _____

Vocabulary in Context **6** In this passage compile means
☐ a. collect.
☐ b. lose.
☐ c. finish.
☐ d. buy. _____

Add your scores for questions 1–6. Enter the total here and on the graph on page 216. Total Score _____

73 Bessie Coleman, Determined Pilot

For the first 10 years after the Wright brothers' original flight in 1903, flying was only a sport. It was a pastime for daredevils. One very determined daredevil was Bessie Coleman. She was the first black woman to fly an airplane.

Coleman, born in Texas in 1892, the tenth of 13 children, dreamed of being a pilot. To earn money for flying lessons, she washed other people's laundry. At the age of 19 she took a train to Chicago, where she enrolled in a beauty school. For five years she worked in a barbershop, and then she looked for a flying school. There were none in the United States that would teach women, but Coleman heard that there were schools in France that would. So she studied the language and sailed off to France.

When she returned to the United States in 1921, Coleman was the first licensed black woman pilot. Her "aerial acrobatic <u>exhibitions</u>" dazzled audiences. She took her airplane through loop-the-loops. She did slow rolls and sharp rolls. She did tail-spins and flew upside down. Audiences were amazed when she performed a move called "falling leaf."

Coleman became a celebrity. She performed her acrobatic flights all over the country. She also spoke to African-American audiences in schools, churches, and theaters. Fly, she told them. Be a part of the new aviation industry. Many young African-American men listened to her. Some became honored military pilots during World War II. Many others made their careers in aviation.

On April 29, 1926, Coleman was flying when a tool carelessly left in the airplane cockpit jammed the control stick. The plane went into a dive and did not recover. The daring 34-year-old pilot was killed.

Main Idea 1

	Answer	Score
Mark the *main idea*	M	15
Mark the statement that is *too broad*	B	5
Mark the statement that is *too narrow*	N	5

a. Many early pilots were daredevils.	☐	_____
b. Women could learn to fly in France.	☐	_____
c. Bessie Coleman was a pioneer in the aviation industry.	☐	_____

Score 15 points for each correct answer.   Score

Subject Matter   2   The focus of this passage is mainly

☐ a. French history.

☐ b. United States history.

☐ c. World War II history.

☐ d. aviation history.   _____

Supporting Details   3   Bessie Coleman went to France to

☐ a. speak to African-American audiences.

☐ b. learn to fly.

☐ c. go to beauty school.

☐ d. learn French.   _____

Conclusion   4   Bessie Coleman's life teaches which of the following lessons?

☐ a. Become a celebrity.

☐ b. Flying is a pastime for daredevils.

☐ c. Follow your dreams.

☐ d. Learn French.   _____

Clarifying Devices   5   Which of the following is an "aerial acrobatic"?

☐ a. flying upside down

☐ b. speaking to audiences

☐ c. getting a pilot's license

☐ d. dazzling audiences   _____

Vocabulary in Context   6   The word <u>exhibition</u> means

☐ a. a holding back.

☐ b. outside of Earth's atmosphere.

☐ c. a public show.

☐ d. the amount of money spent.   _____

Add your scores for questions 1–6. Enter the total here and on the graph on page 216.   Total Score   _____

74 The Fastest Answer

Carl Friedrich Gauss, one of the most famous of all mathematicians, was born in Germany in 1777. Gauss made contributions to physics and astronomy as well as to mathematics. He was a child <u>prodigy</u>, making many important discoveries before the age of 20. As early as three years old, Gauss corrected his father's math when he was adding a series of long computations.

In his later years Gauss liked to tell a story from his school days. When he was 10, he entered his first arithmetic class. The teacher was particularly strict, perhaps even cruel. In one beginning class he gave the boys a very difficult addition problem, a list of 100 numbers to be added. The problem may have looked like this:

$$4897 + 4970 + 5043 + \ldots + 12{,}124$$

At that time, school boys did their math on small slates using chalk. The first boy to solve a problem was to lay his slate on the teacher's desk. As each boy finished, he added to the stack of slates. The teacher had barely finished writing the problem when Gauss wrote down the answer and laid his slate on the desk. As the other boys worked on the problem for the next hour, Gauss sat quietly and ignored the sarcastic glances from his teacher. Of course Gauss had the right answer; in fact, he was the only student who got the long and difficult problem correct.

How did he do it? He had looked at the numbers and seen a pattern in them. In this case each number to be added was 73 more than the preceding number. In any series of this type, a formula can be applied to the numbers to quickly arrive at a solution. Although the formula is a rather simple part of mathematics, the child Gauss made the initial discovery of it at the age of 10!

Main Idea	1		Answer	Score
	Mark the *main idea*		M	15
	Mark the statement that is *too broad*		B	5
	Mark the statement that is *too narrow*		N	5

a. The mathematician Gauss showed his talents at a very early age. ☐ _____

b. Gauss added the series of large numbers quickly. ☐ _____

c. Some mathematicians are remarkably intelligent. ☐ _____

Score 15 points for each correct answer.   **Score**

Subject Matter **2** This passage is mostly concerned with
- ☐ a. the contributions Gauss made to mathematics.
- ☐ b. an early incident in the life of Gauss.
- ☐ c. how to add a long series of numbers.
- ☐ d. methods of education in the 1700s.   _____

Supporting Details **3** Gauss solved the difficult math problem by
- ☐ a. using a computer.
- ☐ b. making a diagram.
- ☐ c. carefully adding all the numbers.
- ☐ d. figuring out a formula.   _____

Conclusion **4** Gauss's teacher probably assumed that
- ☐ a. students would solve the problem by cheating.
- ☐ b. everyone in the class enjoyed math.
- ☐ c. it would take all the students a long time to solve the problem.
- ☐ d. few of the students knew how to add.   _____

Clarifying Devices **5** The writer describes Gauss's amazing talents by
- ☐ a. relating a story.
- ☐ b. explaining a math problem.
- ☐ c. comparing him to other mathematicians.
- ☐ d. describing his key discoveries.   _____

Vocabulary in Context **6** The word prodigy means a
- ☐ a. student.
- ☐ b. very brilliant young person.
- ☐ c. teacher.
- ☐ d. parent.   _____

Add your scores for questions 1–6. Enter the total here and on the graph on page 216.   **Total Score**   _____

75 Science Fiction

If you've seen movies like *Independence Day,* you probably have an idea what science fiction is. But you may think it is something made for the movies. Actually, science fiction is considerably older than that.

Here are some facts about science fiction. It tells stories that use scientific facts or ideas. Often the stories are set in the future. Sometimes, though, they are set in the present, only a different kind of present than really exists. (For example, maybe the present-day world is run entirely by machines.) The locations of science fiction stories can vary too. Many are set on Earth. But some are set on distant planets.

Jules Verne was an early science fiction writer. He wrote in the mid-1800s. In one of his books, *Twenty Thousand Leagues Under the Sea,* he described travel in a submarine years before one was invented. H. G. Wells also wrote in the nineteenth century. In his book *The Time Machine* a man from his own time traveled far into the future. He criticized the society there, which reminded him in many ways of his own society.

The twentieth century also had great science fiction writers. Ray Bradbury wrote many stories about the future. Sometimes—as in *The Martian Chronicles*—these were set on other planets. One book by Arthur C. Clarke, *Childhood's End,* was about an alien invasion that seemed to change the world for the better. Author Ursula LeGuin made up strange new planets. She wrote of the beings and societies that existed there.

Science fiction writers are usually doing more than just trying to amuse their readers. They are <u>speculating</u> on what future technology might be like. Or they are thinking about how people would act if the world changed drastically—say, from a nuclear explosion. Good science fiction gives the reader serious ideas to think about.

Main Idea	1	Answer	Score
	Mark the *main idea*	M	15
	Mark the statement that is *too broad*	B	5
	Mark the statement that is *too narrow*	N	5

a. Great science fiction writers present views of a unique present or an unusual future. ☐ _____

b. One of the earliest science fiction writers was Jules Verne. ☐ _____

c. Science fiction isn't just something you find in movies. ☐ _____

Score 15 points for each correct answer.   Score

Subject Matter   2   This passage is mostly about
        ☐ a. why science fiction is so popular.
        ☐ b. the things famous science fiction writers
            wrote about.
        ☐ c. the difference between science fiction
            movies and science fiction books.
        ☐ d. Jules Verne and H. G. Wells.   _____

Supporting   3   Some of Ursula LeGuin's books are about
Details   ☐ a. Mars.
        ☐ b. travel to the future.
        ☐ c. submarines.
        ☐ d. imaginary planets.   _____

Conclusion   4   The author seems to think that reading science
      fiction is
        ☐ a. difficult.
        ☐ b. a waste of time.
        ☐ c. a way to learn about science.
        ☐ d. worthwhile.   _____

Clarifying   5   The author begins by mentioning the movie
Devices   *Independence Day* in order to
        ☐ a. make you feel comfortable by starting with
            something familiar.
        ☐ b. prove how similar the movie is to books.
        ☐ c. show that the passage will be mostly about
            movies.
        ☐ d. challenge you.   _____

Vocabulary   6   In this passage <u>speculating</u> means
in Context   ☐ a. gambling.
        ☐ b. coming up with theories.
        ☐ c. looking through reading glasses.
        ☐ d. ignoring.   _____

Add your scores for questions 1–6. Enter the total here   **Total**
and on the graph on page 216.   **Score**   _____

76 Sources of Energy

In our lives, we enjoy everything from computers to cars to heated buildings. These comforts have something in common: they all need energy to work. Energy has many different forms. One form, electricity, comes mostly from steam-powered generators. Steam is made by burning coal, oil, or natural gas. Gasoline is another form of energy. Gasoline is made from oil. Oil has many other uses. Paints, fertilizers, and plastics are made from it. We even use it to heat buildings. Coal, oil, and gas are natural resources. We take them from nature to make our lives easier.

We can classify natural resources as either renewable or nonrenewable. Coal, oil, and gas are nonrenewable. They take millions of years to form. Some scientists predict that we will run out of oil and gas in 50 to 100 years. Coal is more plentiful. So it may last for hundreds of years. Resources such as wood and water are renewable. They can be grown or recycled naturally. They can, however, become limited from overuse.

We have developed some alternate sources of energy. But these sources have drawbacks. For example, hydroelectric power, or energy from running water, affects the ecology of surrounding areas. Nuclear power, another alternate source, presents the threat of nuclear accidents. There are also problems related to the storage of nuclear wastes. Solar and wind energies aren't consistent. We can't rely on them. Geothermal energy, caused by heat from inside the earth, is tapped by drawing steam and hot water from pools and geysers. This energy source, like most others, isn't fully developed.

It's time to get serious about energy. We must find practical, alternate energy sources. If we wait too long, it will be too late. We will run out of coal, oil, and natural gas. Then we won't have the resources to make alternate energy sources.

Main Idea	1	Answer	Score
Mark the *main idea*		M	15
Mark the statement that is *too broad*		B	5
Mark the statement that is *too narrow*		N	5

a. People enjoy many comforts in their daily lives. ☐ _____

b. Coal, oil, and natural gas are nonrenewable resources. ☐ _____

c. People must get serious about developing alternate sources of energy. ☐ _____

Subject Matter 2 This passage is mainly about
- [ ] a. putting natural resources into categories.
- [ ] b. renewable and nonrenewable resources.
- [ ] c. energy sources and why we need new ones.
- [ ] d. using geothermal energy.

_____

Supporting Details 3 Oil and natural gas
- [ ] a. form in the ground in just a few years.
- [ ] b. are nonrenewable resources that we may soon use up.
- [ ] c. may be available for hundreds of years.
- [ ] d. are found on every continent.

_____

Conclusion 4 The second paragraph suggests that renewable resources
- [ ] a. take millions of years to form.
- [ ] b. cannot be grown or recycled.
- [ ] c. will last for hundreds of years.
- [ ] d. will become scarce if we don't start using them wisely.

_____

Clarifying Devices 5 In discussing "alternate forms of energy," the writer
- [ ] a. tells what is good about them.
- [ ] b. points out the problems with them.
- [ ] c. focuses mostly on oil and gas.
- [ ] d. lists places where they may be found.

_____

Vocabulary in Context 6 <u>Drawbacks</u> are
- [ ] a. pictures.
- [ ] b. shortcomings.
- [ ] c. sources of energy.
- [ ] d. warnings.

_____

Add your scores for questions 1–6. Enter the total here and on the graph on page 217.

Total Score

_____

77 What Is Psychology?

Why do human beings behave as they do? This is something people have always wondered. Aristotle, an ancient Greek thinker, said the mind was separate from the body. He wanted to know what the mind could do. *Psychology* comes from two Greek words. One is *psyche,* meaning "mind." The other is *logia,* meaning "study." So psychology is "the study of the mind."

In the Middle Ages, <u>scholars</u> studied people's behavior from a religious viewpoint rather than looking at what the mind could do. In the 1600s and 1700s, other views became important. Some scholars believed as Aristotle did—that the mind and body are separate. They believed the mind can think and reason at birth. Others said the mind is empty at birth. They said that knowledge comes from the senses and that ideas come from experience.

In the 1800s German researchers began to study the mind in a scientific way. Then an American set up the first lab where experiments on the mind could be performed. Psychology became its own field of study.

Today psychology is one of the social sciences. It studies behavior and how the mind works. Psychologists observe people, conduct experiments, and record what they see. They look for patterns to help them understand and predict behavior.

When psychologists work with people, they ask questions about thoughts, feelings, and actions. The answers can help people better understand their own personalities. They can help people change habits and sometimes even find ways to learn better. With psychology, we can begin to answer our first question: Why do human beings behave as they do?

Main Idea	1	Answer	Score
	Mark the *main idea*	M	15
	Mark the statement that is *too broad*	B	5
	Mark the statement that is *too narrow*	N	5
	a. Psychology may be practiced in labs.	☐	___
	b. Psychology studies the mind and behavior.	☐	___
	c. Psychology is a social science.	☐	___

Subject Matter   **2**   This passage is mostly about
- ☐ a. psychology and how it developed.
- ☐ b. famous people who studied psychology.
- ☐ c. why psychology is popular today.
- ☐ d. psychology in the Middle Ages.   _____

Supporting Details   **3**   The first scientific study of the mind was done by
- ☐ a. Greeks.
- ☐ b. Americans.
- ☐ c. Germans.
- ☐ d. the French.   _____

Conclusion   **4**   To practice psychology correctly, a person should
- ☐ a. be familiar with research done by others.
- ☐ b. rely mainly on a desire to help people.
- ☐ c. have an office with a couch in it.
- ☐ d. have personal problems that need to be solved.   _____

Clarifying Devices   **5**   The first three paragraphs of this passage
- ☐ a. give an explanation of psychology.
- ☐ b. tell the history of psychology.
- ☐ c. show how psychology helps people.
- ☐ d. ask questions about psychology.   _____

Vocabulary in Context   **6**   In this passage, a <u>scholar</u> is someone
- ☐ a. who owns a school.
- ☐ b. from Nova Scotia.
- ☐ c. with a lot of knowledge.
- ☐ d. who works for the church.   _____

Add your scores for questions 1–6. Enter the total here and on the graph on page 217.   **Total Score**   _____

78 Working with Interest Rates

When you put money in a bank account, your money earns interest. This interest is a payment from the bank for the use of your money. The bank may pay you any interest rate it desires; these days the usual rate is around 5 percent. The basic formula for figuring out how much interest you will earn on an investment is fairly simple. To figure the interest, multiply three things: the **p**rincipal (or amount you invest), the interest **r**ate put into decimal form (5 percent would be written .05), and the **t**ime in years. The formula can be written as $i = prt$.

The formula $i = prt$ is for simple interest. It does not help you find interest that is compounded. Compounding occurs when you leave your money alone. Then every so often the interest is computed again using a new principal. The formula for compound interest lets you find the value of an investment after some number of years. However, it is a fairly complex formula. If you want to work with it, you'll need a scientific calculator with an exponent key.

Most people find the compound interest formula <u>perplexing</u>. They ask a bank or other investment service to do the math for them. But there is a simple way to figure out when your money will double in value. This is called the "Rule of 72." If you divide the annual interest rate into 72, the answer is the number of years it will take to double your savings. So money invested at 5 percent will take more than 14 years to double (72 divided by 5).

Now here is a question to ponder. What happens if p equals zero? If you put that value for p into the formula, the answer will be zero. In other words, if you invest no principal, you'll get no interest. And although this is the simplest math of all, it is not a good long-term investment strategy!

Main Idea	1		
		Answer	**Score**
	Mark the *main idea*	M	15
	Mark the statement that is *too broad*	B	5
	Mark the statement that is *too narrow*	N	5
	a. Calculating interest from investments is based on formulas and rules.	☐	_____
	b. Compound interest formulas are very complicated.	☐	_____
	c. Investment strategies require math.	☐	_____

Subject Matter   **2**   This passage is mostly about
- ☐ a. understanding mathematical formulas.
- ☐ b. why saving money is important.
- ☐ c. ways to figure out how much money you are earning in a bank account.
- ☐ d. using a scientific calculator.

       _____

Supporting Details   **3**   The "Rule of 72" helps you find the
- ☐ a. current interest rate.
- ☐ b. interest you get after 72 years.
- ☐ c. amount of money you should invest.
- ☐ d. number of years it takes an investment to double in value.

       _____

Conclusion   **4**   At 7 percent annual interest, an investment will double in about
- ☐ a. 10 months.
- ☐ b. 10 years.
- ☐ c. 72 months.
- ☐ d. 72 years.

       _____

Clarifying Devices   **5**   Letters are underlined in three words in the first paragraph in order to show that
- ☐ a. the letters are part of the interest formula.
- ☐ b. the letters should be capitalized.
- ☐ c. the words they are in are spelled incorrectly.
- ☐ d. each letter stands for a number.

       _____

Vocabulary in Context   **6**   <u>Perplexing</u> means
- ☐ a. unnecessary.
- ☐ b. long.
- ☐ c. confusing.
- ☐ d. involving percents.

       _____

Add your scores for questions 1–6. Enter the total here and on the graph on page 217.   **Total Score**   _____

79 The Man from Stratford

He lived in the 16th century. A few things, but not really that many, are known about his life. And yet around the world the verdict is <u>unanimous</u>: he was the greatest writer who ever lived. His name was William Shakespeare.

Shakespeare was born in 1564 in a little town called Stratford-on-Avon. When he was in his twenties, he made his way to London. There he spent most of his working life. The theater was very popular at that time, and soon Shakespeare was writing plays. He belonged to an acting company called the Lord Chamberlain's Men and wrote plays for them. (He also acted in some of the plays.) In 1599 the company built the famous Globe Theater. There Shakespeare wrote and acted until he retired in about 1607.

Shakespeare wrote three kinds of plays: comedies, tragedies, and histories. Many of the comedies involved mistaken identities, women pretending to be men, and slapstick situations. One of his famous comedies is *A Midsummer Night's Dream*. Shakespeare's tragedies often were about a noble and honorable man who had one fault that helped bring about his downfall. *Hamlet* is an example. Shakespeare's histories were usually about kings of England, such as *Richard III* or *Henry V*.

What made Shakespeare's work so great? It was not necessarily his stories. Many were retellings of stories the audience already knew. But the way he told the stories was often remarkable. He understood the way people thought and acted, and he built this into his characters. Even though they were created 400 years ago, Shakespeare's characters are believable today.

Shakespeare's use of language—such as his beautiful descriptions and his clear, to-the-point statements—also made him great. Hundreds of famous English quotes come from his plays. One example: "Cowards die many times before their deaths."

Main Idea	1			
			Answer	**Score**
	Mark the *main idea*		M	15
	Mark the statement that is *too broad*		B	5
	Mark the statement that is *too narrow*		N	5
	a. Many plays were written in the 1500s.		☐	_____
	b. Shakespeare was the world's greatest writer.		☐	_____
	c. Shakespeare's plays contain hundreds of well-known statements.		☐	_____

Subject Matter   **2**   This passage gives an overview of
        ☐ a. the Globe Theater.
        ☐ b. theater in the 1500s.
        ☐ c. Shakespeare's histories.
        ☐ d. Shakespeare's life and work.   _____

Supporting   **3**   Many of Shakespeare's plays
Details   ☐ a. were based on original stories.
        ☐ b. were based on stories already familiar to
           the audience.
        ☐ c. were a mixture of comedy and tragedy.
        ☐ d. do not exist today.   _____

Conclusion   **4**   Based on Shakespeare's experience, it is probably
true that members of the Lord Chamberlain's Men
        ☐ a. performed more than one job.
        ☐ b. were jealous of each other.
        ☐ c. could not read or write.
        ☐ d. were all quite young.   _____

Clarifying   **5**   The general organization of this passage is
Devices   ☐ a. Shakespeare's works, greatness, life.
        ☐ b. Shakespeare's life, works, greatness.
        ☐ c. Shakespeare's childhood, works, retirement.
        ☐ d. Shakespeare's greatness, works, life.   _____

Vocabulary   **6**   Unanimous means
in Context   ☐ a. cause for argument.
        ☐ b. surprising.
        ☐ c. kept in written records.
        ☐ d. agreed on by everyone.   _____

**Add your scores for questions 1–6. Enter the total here   Total
and on the graph on page 217.   Score**   _____

80 Scientific Classification System

If you collected baseball cards as a child, your collection may have contained hundreds of cards. How did you find one specific card among them all? You might have organized the cards using a method of <u>classification</u>. When you classify things, you group them by their likenesses. For example, baseball cards might be grouped by year, team, or player. You also might use these likenesses to talk to other card collectors. For example, today you might ask a collector, "Do you have a 1999 Chicago Cubs' Sammy Sosa card?" Other collectors know just which card you want by the way you name it.

Living things are classified in a similar way. First, living things are sorted by their likenesses into main groups called *kingdoms*. For example, all animals have these likenesses: they move, and they eat plants or other animals. Because of these similarities, all animals are grouped together. They are in the kingdom Animalia.

Next, the living things in each kingdom are classified into six other groups, each more specific than the last. The chart shows the classification groups for humans.

	Kingdom	Phylum	Class	Order	Family	Genus	Species
Humans	Animalia	Chordata	Mamalia	Primates	Hominidae	*Homo*	*sapiens*

A kingdom is the largest group. A *phylum* is smaller than a kingdom, and a *class* is smaller than a phylum. Since each group is smaller and more specific than the previous one, in a *species,* the smallest group, only things that are very similar are placed. For example, only humans belong to the species *sapiens*. When scientists talk about living things, they name them by their genus and species. Humans belong to genus *Homo* and species *sapiens*. So they are given the scientific name *Homo sapiens*.

Main Idea 1

	Answer	Score
Mark the *main idea*	M	15
Mark the statement that is *too broad*	B	5
Mark the statement that is *too narrow*	N	5

a. The scientific name for humans is *Homo sapiens*. ☐ _____

b. Scientists classify every living thing. ☐ _____

c. A living thing is classified into specific groups by its likenesses. ☐ _____

Subject Matter   **2**   Another good title for this passage would be
- [ ] a. Sammy Sosa and the Chicago Cubs.
- [ ] b. Humans Are Animals Too.
- [ ] c. Grouping by Likenesses.
- [ ] d. The Five Kingdoms.

_____

Supporting Details   **3**   The largest classification group is
- [ ] a. species.
- [ ] b. family.
- [ ] c. class.
- [ ] d. kingdom.

_____

Conclusion   **4**   The last paragraph suggests that scientists
- [ ] a. use the name _Homo sapiens_ when talking about humans.
- [ ] b. communicate frequently about the classification system.
- [ ] c. would be better off naming living things by kingdom and phylum.
- [ ] d. only study large groups of living things.

_____

Clarifying Devices   **5**   The chart in this passage helps the reader to
- [ ] a. read details in chronological order.
- [ ] b. see details in their order of importance.
- [ ] c. identify different scientific categories.
- [ ] d. identify cause and effect relationships.

_____

Vocabulary in Context   **6**   <u>Classification</u> is the process of
- [ ] a. grouping things according to likenesses.
- [ ] b. arranging plants and animals into one group.
- [ ] c. naming all living things.
- [ ] d. sharing information with other scientists.

_____

Add your scores for questions 1–6. Enter the total here and on the graph on page 217.   **Total Score**

_____

81 The First Written Records

No computers, no calculators, no paper and pencil. Before writing, people's memories were the containers for storing knowledge. But in ancient Mesopotamia, the Sumerians were about to invent the first writing. The time was more than 4,000 years ago.

Many Sumerians were merchants and traders. They traded grain, dates, wool, and dairy products for tools and building supplies. The Sumerians needed to keep track of all this trading. At first they used clay or stone tokens in a clay jar called a *bulla*. The marks they made on the outside of the bulla may have led to the invention of writing. Their first written symbols were pictures of the things they traded. Later, the pictures stood for syllables. Soon the Sumerians were combining those syllables into words.

Around 3000 B.C., the pictures were drawn more simply. Another type of writing <u>emerged</u> called cuneiform. This writing could be done easily on wet clay. The marks were written in the clay with a narrow reed or stick and were shaped like a triangle. Cuneiform had 600 symbols. With cuneiform, people could record the histories of the wars they fought. They could even write poems. Cuneiform was used in the Middle East for about 2,000 years.

Modern people could not read cuneiform. But in the 1800s, an important translation was made by Sir Henry Creswicke Rawlinson. He translated some ancient writing that was found in Iran. His translation led to an understanding of ancient cuneiform. Archaeologists today continue to translate the first writings. Each translation gives more information about ancient people.

Main Idea	1			
			Answer	**Score**
	Mark the *main idea*		M	15
	Mark the statement that is *too broad*		B	5
	Mark the statement that is *too narrow*		N	5
	a. The Sumerians were an ancient people.		☐	_____
	b. The Sumerians traded items like grain and wool.		☐	_____
	c. The first writing was invented by the Sumerians.		☐	_____

Subject Matter   2   This passage is mostly about
  ☐ a. Sumerian culture.
  ☐ b. the development of early writing.
  ☐ c. why trade was important in ancient civilizations.
  ☐ d. Sir Henry Creswicke Rawlinson.   _____

Supporting Details   3   Cuneiform contained
  ☐ a. pictures of things that were traded.
  ☐ b. an alphabet similar to the one we use today.
  ☐ c. syllables and words.
  ☐ d. about 600 symbols.   _____

Conclusion   4   Writing developed because people
  ☐ a. wanted to read books.
  ☐ b. had a need to keep records.
  ☐ c. were not good at drawing pictures.
  ☐ d. had poor memories.   _____

Clarifying Devices   5   In the first paragraph, "people's memories were the containers for storing knowledge" is
  ☐ a. a simile.
  ☐ b. a metaphor.
  ☐ c. a rhyme.
  ☐ d. personification.   _____

Vocabulary in Context   6   The word <u>emerged</u> means
  ☐ a. went under.
  ☐ b. needed help.
  ☐ c. came forth.
  ☐ d. vanished.   _____

Add your scores for questions 1–6. Enter the total here and on the graph on page 217.   **Total Score**   _____

82 The Bridges of Königsberg

The city of Königsberg, Germany, has seven bridges and a river. The bridges connect an island with other parts of the town. For many years people argued about the bridges. Was it possible to walk through the city and cross each bridge only once? Many people tried it. But they either skipped a bridge or crossed a bridge more than once.

The Swiss mathematician Leonhard Euler heard about the puzzle of the bridges. He thought it was an interesting problem. Euler <u>reduced</u> the problem to its most basic elements. He drew a diagram that showed only the seven bridges. Such a diagram is called a *network*. Then he tried to trace the diagram with a pencil without retracing any part of it.

Here is a network showing the bridges of Königsberg. There are seven heavy dark bands, one for each bridge. It is much easier to try to trace the network with a pencil than to walk around the city trying to find a route over the bridges.

Euler was able to prove that there is no solution to the problem. A route that included each bridge once and only once was impossible. As Euler worked on the problem, he discovered other more general things about networks. He wrote several important theorems that mathematicians use to analyze all types of networks.

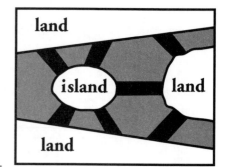

Today networks are used to represent many kinds of situations. The part of mathematics that began with the puzzle of the Königsberg bridges may now be helping you to make a long distance telephone call or to sign on to the Internet.

Main Idea 1 ────────────────────

	Answer	Score
Mark the *main idea*	M	15
Mark the statement that is *too broad*	B	5
Mark the statement that is *too narrow*	N	5

a. Königsberg has seven bridges. ☐ ____

b. The mathematics of networks began with a puzzle about bridges. ☐ ____

c. Networks may help you make a long distance call. ☐ ____

Score 15 points for each correct answer.   Score

Subject Matter   **2** This passage is mostly concerned with
- [ ] a. the life of the mathematician Leonhard Euler.
- [ ] b. the city of Königsberg, Germany.
- [ ] c. networks and how they are used.
- [ ] d. why some math problems have no solution.   _____

Supporting Details   **3** Leonhard Euler used a network to prove that
- [ ] a. all networks have seven lines.
- [ ] b. the bridges could not be crossed only once in one trip across the city.
- [ ] c. the problem of the bridges was incorrectly stated.
- [ ] d. networks are needed for telephone cables.   _____

Conclusion   **4** In the network diagram, the gray areas stand for
- [ ] a. bridges.
- [ ] b. the river.
- [ ] c. a road.
- [ ] d. land.   _____

Clarifying Devices   **5** In the first paragraph the writer introduces the concept of networks by
- [ ] a. explaining a mathematical diagram.
- [ ] b. giving a short biography of Leonhard Euler.
- [ ] c. describing an old puzzle about bridges.
- [ ] d. relating networks to telephone cable systems.   _____

Vocabulary in Context   **6** In this passage reduced means
- [ ] a. simplified.
- [ ] b. lost weight.
- [ ] c. lessened the amount of.
- [ ] d. figured out again.   _____

Add your scores for questions 1–6. Enter the total here and on the graph on page 217.   Total Score   _____

83 Arts and Crafts Houses

Do you live in a bungalow? Do you know anyone who does? A bungalow is a house style made popular during the Arts and Crafts Movement. This movement influenced American design and architecture about 100 years ago.

The leaders of the Arts and Crafts Movement were looking for change. They saw two things happening around them. One was that industry and things made by machine seemed to be taking over the world. The other was that people were building very elaborate houses with cramped rooms and useless ornamentation.

Leaders of the movement wanted to build simple, comfortable houses. They wanted homes that middle-class people could live in and enjoy. They looked to nature for inspiration. This meant using lots of natural materials such as wood and stone.

Many Arts and Crafts houses were bungalows because the style fit in with their builders' beliefs. These buildings were low, usually only one story. They often had wide front porches. The roofs were sloping and seemed to shelter the houses. The interiors were simple and tasteful. Many Arts and Crafts living rooms had stone fireplaces <u>flanked</u> with wooden bookcases or benches. Dining rooms often had built-in china cabinets made of wood. Some builders even decorated the interiors. Wallpapers used simple floral designs. Furniture often had large wooden frames. The preferred colors were from nature—greens, browns, and golds.

Many early Arts and Crafts bungalows were built in California. Soon the style spread across the country. (The Sears, Roebuck catalog even sold house plans and building kits by mail.) The insides, though, often had less detail than the earlier houses. The "simple" bungalow as originally designed had become too costly for the average person that it was supposedly designed for!

Main Idea	1		
		Answer	**Score**
	Mark the *main idea*	M	15
	Mark the statement that is *too broad*	B	5
	Mark the statement that is *too narrow*	N	5

a. Arts and Crafts was an architectural movement. ☐ _____

b. Bungalows were a characteristic house of the Arts and Crafts Movement. ☐ _____

c. Arts and Crafts builders designed interiors as well as exteriors. ☐ _____

Score 15 points for each correct answer.   Score

Subject Matter   **2**   Another good title for this passage would be
- ☐ a. Bungalows and the Arts and Crafts Movement.
- ☐ b. Interiors and Exteriors.
- ☐ c. Why People Like Bungalows.
- ☐ d. Arts and Crafts in California.   _____

Supporting Details   **3**   Arts and Crafts builders wanted to
- ☐ a. show off to other builders.
- ☐ b. build houses with natural materials.
- ☐ c. use a lot of ornamentation.
- ☐ d. build only in warm climates like California.   _____

Conclusion   **4**   In decorating an interior, an Arts and Crafts builder would most likely include
- ☐ a. aluminum chairs.
- ☐ b. elaborate chandeliers
- ☐ c. stainless steel tables.
- ☐ d. earth-color rugs and vases.   _____

Clarifying Devices   **5**   The writer mentions Sears, Roebuck in order to
- ☐ a. show how popular bungalows had become.
- ☐ b. show that anything could be bought from a catalog.
- ☐ c. take you back into United States history.
- ☐ d. show why Sears is still successful.   _____

Vocabulary in Context   **6**   In this passage the word <u>flanked</u> means
- ☐ a. covered with paint.
- ☐ b. blocked by.
- ☐ c. set at the sides of.
- ☐ d. wooden.   _____

Add your scores for questions 1–6. Enter the total here and on the graph on page 217.   **Total Score**   _____

84 Climate

Are you planning a vacation? If you like hot and extremely dry summers, go to Phoenix, Arizona. For hot temperatures but lots of rain and thunderstorms, try Miami, Florida. If you want average temperatures and rainfall, St. Louis, Missouri, is the spot. Or if you're a cold weather fan, head to Fairbanks, Alaska. Its winters are very cold with very little precipitation. Each of these cities has a certain type of weather. The average weather for a place over many years is called *climate,* and in no two places in the world is it exactly the same. How can this be?

Many things in nature, such as sunshine, temperature, and precipitation, affect climate. Nearness to mountains, oceans, and large lakes affects it too. Another factor is <u>altitude</u>, or height above sea level. Air cools as altitude increases. So a city at a higher altitude may be colder than one at a lower altitude. Finally, winds affect climate. They move heat and moisture between the oceans and continents. Winds keep the tropics from overheating. They keep the polar regions from getting overly cold.

Climate changes over long periods of time. Some scientists think, for example, that the earth's climate changed at the time of the dinosaurs. They think the dinosaurs died because of the change. What causes a climate to change? One possible cause may be changes in the sun. Sunspots, for example, are cool, dark spots that form on the sun. Sunspots may decrease precipitation on the earth and cause unusually dry periods. Changes in the atmosphere may change climate too. Volcanic eruptions, for instance, release solid particles into the air. These particles may form a cloud that blocks out the sun's heat. Human activity is another cause of climate change. Air pollution and the reduction of forest cover may have long-term effects on climate.

Main Idea	1		
		Answer	**Score**
	Mark the *main idea*	M	15
	Mark the statement that is *too broad*	B	5
	Mark the statement that is *too narrow*	N	5
	a. Climate varies from place to place.	☐	_____
	b. The climate of Phoenix is hot and extremely dry.	☐	_____
	c. Climate is a long-term pattern of weather, but some things can change it.	☐	_____

Subject Matter 2 This passage is concerned with things that affect
- ☐ a. precipitation.
- ☐ b. climate.
- ☐ c. altitude.
- ☐ d. sunspots.   _____

Supporting Details 3 Change in climate may have caused
- ☐ a. dinosaurs to die.
- ☐ b. dark spots to form on the sun.
- ☐ c. volcanic eruptions.
- ☐ d. air pollution.   _____

Conclusion 4 The effect of a volcanic eruption on climate may be to make it
- ☐ a. wetter.
- ☐ b. dryer.
- ☐ c. warmer.
- ☐ d. colder.   _____

Clarifying Devices 5 To help readers understand how climate can change, the writer uses
- ☐ a. examples.
- ☐ b. a story about the seashore.
- ☐ c. order of importance.
- ☐ d. a strong argument.   _____

Vocabulary in Context 6 Which of the following is the place of greatest <u>altitude</u> on a mountain?
- ☐ a. the foot of the mountain
- ☐ b. 8,500 feet up the mountain
- ☐ c. the top of the mountain
- ☐ d. 15,785 feet up the mountain   _____

Add your scores for questions 1–6. Enter the total here and on the graph on page 217.   Total Score   _____

85 The Better Buy

Many consumer products that you buy frequently come in more than one size. We all assume that you save money if you buy the largest size you can use, and most of the time this assumption turns out to be true. Sometimes, however, the savings may not be <u>significant</u>. So before you automatically reach for the largest size of some product, you might want to do a little math.

Assume a product comes in two sizes: the smaller size has 24 ounces and costs $1.19; the larger size is 36 ounces for $1.69. To find the savings, if any, on the larger size, you can compute the unit price. (Units are ounces, pounds, or whatever measure the product is sold in.) In this case, the unit price is the cost per ounce for each size, so use a calculator to divide the price by the number of ounces.

24 ounces for $1.19 $1.19 ÷ 24 ounces = 0.0495 = 4.95¢ per ounce
36 ounces for $1.69 $1.69 ÷ 36 ounces = 0.0469 = 4.69¢ per ounce

You can see that the 36 ounce-size has a lower unit price, so it is the better buy.

But how much do you actually save by buying the larger size? To find out, subtract the two unit prices to compare them: $0.0495 − $0.0469 = $0.0026. In this example, the difference in the unit prices is about $0.003—only three-tenths of a penny! So if you don't really need the larger size of this particular product, you probably shouldn't purchase it. In addition to price, another factor to consider when choosing the size to buy is the expiration date on the product. If you're not likely to use up the larger size before the expiration date, then you should buy a smaller size.

The next time you go to the supermarket, take a pocket calculator with you and try finding the unit prices on different sizes of some products. You may very well discover that a *smaller* size offers you the best value!

Main Idea   1

	Answer	Score
Mark the *main idea*	M	15
Mark the statement that is *too broad*	B	5
Mark the statement that is *too narrow*	N	5

a. A pocket calculator can help in computing the unit price. ☐ _____

b. Mathematics can help consumers. ☐ _____

c. Computing unit prices helps you compare costs. ☐ _____

Subject Matter   **2**   This passage is mainly about
- ☐ a. using a calculator.
- ☐ b. comparison shopping.
- ☐ c. balancing a household budget.
- ☐ d. dividing decimals.   _____

Supporting Details   **3**   To compute a unit price, you should
- ☐ a. first change ounces to pounds.
- ☐ b. subtract two numbers.
- ☐ c. divide the price by the expiration date.
- ☐ d. divide the price by the number of units.   _____

Conclusion   **4**   It is reasonable to conclude that you
- ☐ a. never save money buying a larger size.
- ☐ b. always save money buying a larger size.
- ☐ c. may not save much money buying a larger size.
- ☐ d. usually don't use a product before it expires.   _____

Clarifying Devices   **5**   The writer shows how to compare prices for
- ☐ a. two different sizes of the same product.
- ☐ b. two different brands of the same product.
- ☐ c. products without price labels.
- ☐ d. products that are sold at farmers' markets.   _____

Vocabulary in Context   **6**   In this passage the word <u>significant</u> means
- ☐ a. able to be printed on a sign.
- ☐ b. practical.
- ☐ c. large enough to make a difference.
- ☐ d. important.   _____

Add your scores for questions 1–6. Enter the total here and on the graph on page 217.   **Total Score**   _____

86 The Beginnings of Democracy

Democracy, or rule by all the people, is often upheld as an <u>ideal</u> form of government. Democracy began in ancient Greece, but it developed slowly.

Before there was democracy, the people of Greece came under other forms of rule. First there was monarchy, in which a king ruled over the people. During the Dark Age of Greece, most Greek city-states were ruled by monarchy. Next there was oligarchy. Here a small group of people ruled over everyone else. At the end of the Dark Age, a small group of nobles shared power with the king. Then during the sixth century B.C., there were problems with oligarchies. This led to the rise of tyrants. Even though a tyrant seizes power by force, the Greek people supported tyrants. The tyrants promised to reform laws and help the poor. Finally, in about 510 B.C., the people had enough of tyrants. They threw them out of power. The people decided to share the power themselves. This was the beginning of democracy.

In the democratic city of Athens, Greece, citizens took part in the government. Not everyone, though, could be a citizen. A citizen had to be male and over the age of 18. Usually a man's father, and sometimes his mother's father, also had to be citizens. Only about 15 percent of the 300,000 people living in Athens could be citizens. Women and children could not, even though they made up 48 percent of the population. Foreigners living in Athens could not, even though they made up 12 percent of the population. Slaves could not, even though they made up 25 percent of the population.

The democracy of the ancient Greeks is not the ideal for which modern countries strive. But the Greeks can take credit for the beginning of an idea.

Main Idea 1

	Answer	Score
Mark the *main idea*	M	15
Mark the statement that is *too broad*	B	5
Mark the statement that is *too narrow*	N	5

a. Democracy began in Greece.	☐	_____
b. Oligarchies led to democracy.	☐	_____
c. Democracy is a form of government.	☐	_____

Subject Matter   **2**   This passage is mainly about
☐ a. the beginnings of democracy.
☐ b. all forms of government.
☐ c. Greek life.
☐ d. oligarchies.   _____

Supporting Details   **3**   People supported tyrants because
☐ a. they were tired of being ruled by a king.
☐ b. tyrants promised democratic rule.
☐ c. tyrants made promises of reform.
☐ d. women could now vote.   _____

Conclusion   **4**   Which statement best summarizes the ideas in this passage?
☐ a. Democracy began in Europe.
☐ b. Democracy caught on quickly everywhere.
☐ c. Early Greek democracy was for all people.
☐ d. The true ideal of democracy was begun but not achieved in ancient Greece.   _____

Clarifying Devices   **5**   The order of ancient Greek governments is indicated by
☐ a. a timeline.
☐ b. the numerals 1, 2, 3, and 4.
☐ c. the words _first, next, then,_ and _finally._
☐ d. a bulleted list.   _____

Vocabulary in Context   **6**   The word <u>ideal</u> in this passage means
☐ a. expensive.
☐ b. perfect.
☐ c. unusual.
☐ d. a thought.   _____

Add your scores for questions 1–6. Enter the total here and on the graph on page 217.   **Total Score**   _____

87 The Founder of Modern Dance

As the 1800s ended, dance, like most other arts, was fairly <u>conventional</u>. If people went to a dance performance, they probably went to a ballet. This dance had precise moves and rigid postures. People enjoyed ballet, and it was widely accepted.

However, at around that time a young woman from San Francisco entered the scene. She would change dance forever. Her name was Isadora Duncan.

Duncan was born into an artistic family. Even as a child she loved dancing and taught dance classes for younger children. She quickly developed some very strong ideas of what dance should be.

Duncan took her inspiration from nature. She loved the Pacific Ocean and the towering pine trees of her native California. She wanted to represent these natural elements in her dances. She also looked at people's natural movements, especially the movements of children. Running, skipping, jumping, kneeling—these were things done by children all over the world. Duncan incorporated them into dance routines. She believed that older dances were rather lifeless; hers, she felt, should express emotion.

When Duncan performed her dances in places like Chicago and New York, she caused a sensation. People were not prepared to see a young woman in a thin, flowing dress running and leaping across the stage barefoot. She had to go to Europe for acceptance. Received more favorably in London, she gradually opened dance schools in many cities. Soon she was touring and performing everywhere. Her ideas paved the way for what we know as modern dance today.

Duncan's death was as startling as her life. As she rode in an open sports car in France, the long scarf around her neck tangled in the car's wheels and she was strangled.

Main Idea	1		
		Answer	**Score**
	Mark the *main idea*	M	15
	Mark the statement that is *too broad*	B	5
	Mark the statement that is *too narrow*	N	5

a. Dance changed a lot in the early twentieth century. ☐ _____

b. Duncan's ideas about movement and form revolutionized dance. ☐ _____

c. Duncan died in an unusual manner. ☐ _____

174

Subject Matter   **2**   This passage is mostly about
     ☐ a. Isadora Duncan's early life.
     ☐ b. Isadora Duncan's contributions to dance.
     ☐ c. why people in the 1800s liked ballet.
     ☐ d. Isadora Duncan's death.   _____

Supporting   **3**   Duncan got her best early acceptance in
Details
     ☐ a. Chicago.
     ☐ b. San Francisco.
     ☐ c. New York.
     ☐ d. London.   _____

Conclusion   **4**   Early audiences found Duncan's performances
     ☐ a. foolish.
     ☐ b. boring.
     ☐ c. worthwhile.
     ☐ d. scandalous.   _____

Clarifying   **5**   The word *However* at the beginning of the
Devices   second paragraph signals
     ☐ a. that similar information is to follow.
     ☐ b. an argument.
     ☐ c. a contrast.
     ☐ d. a description.   _____

Vocabulary   **6**   In this passage <u>conventional</u> means
in Context
     ☐ a. normal and usual.
     ☐ b. strange and exotic.
     ☐ c. involving a large meeting of people.
     ☐ d. involving people from many different
       professions.   _____

Add your scores for questions 1–6. Enter the total here   **Total**
and on the graph on page 217.   **Score**   _____

88 Cell Structure

You are an <u>organism</u>. Some organisms consist of only a single living cell, but humans are made of trillions of living cells. Like you, many plants and animals are also made of numerous living cells. The diagram below shows the main parts of an animal cell—see if you can identify them as you read.

A cell is covered by a thin layer called a *cell membrane*. The cell membrane has pores, or small openings, in it that allow food and other substances to enter and leave the cell. A jellylike substance called *cytoplasm* fills the inside of a cell. The parts of the cell float in the cytoplasm.

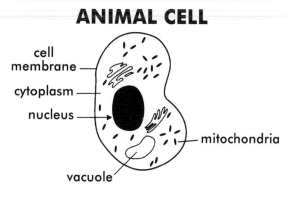

Each part of the cell performs a specific function. Near the center of the cell is the *nucleus,* the "control center" of the cell. It contains information that directs all cellular activities. *Chromosomes* inside the nucleus carry the directions for making new cells. The nucleus is covered by the *nuclear membrane*. It contains pores to let food and other substances in and out of the nucleus. The sausage-shaped *mitochondria* change food materials into energy for the cell. *Vacuoles* store food and water.

Main Idea	1	Answer	Score
	Mark the *main idea*	M	15
	Mark the statement that is *too broad*	B	5
	Mark the statement that is *too narrow*	N	5

a. The various parts of a cell all have their own jobs to do. ☐ ____

b. The nucleus controls activities in the other parts of the cell. ☐ ____

c. Humans are made of trillions of cells. ☐ ____

Subject Matter   **2**   Another good title for this passage would be
- ☐ a. How to Change Food into Energy.
- ☐ b. The Mystery of Pores.
- ☐ c. The Transportation System of a Cell.
- ☐ d. How a Cell Works.   _____

Supporting Details   **3**   The special job of vacuoles is to
- ☐ a. let food in and out of the nucleus.
- ☐ b. make new cells.
- ☐ c. allow substances into and out of the cell.
- ☐ d. store food amd water.   _____

Conclusion   **4**   The arrow on the cell diagram points to
- ☐ a. the cell membrane.
- ☐ b. the nucleus.
- ☐ c. one of the mitochondria.
- ☐ d. one of the vacuoles.   _____

Clarifying Devices   **5**   The term "control center" in the final paragraph suggests that the nucleus functions like
- ☐ a. an airport tower.
- ☐ b. a traffic jam.
- ☐ c. a bus.
- ☐ d. any vehicle with wheels.   _____

Vocabulary in Context   **6**   An <u>organism</u> is a
- ☐ a. musical instrument.
- ☐ b. mixture of dead plants and animals.
- ☐ c. nonliving substance.
- ☐ d. living thing.   _____

Add your scores for questions 1–6. Enter the total here and on the graph on page 217.   **Total Score**   _____

89 Bits and Bytes

Even though the workings of computers appear complicated, in its simplest essence a computer only understands two things—on and off. So all information is presented to the computer in terms of just two digits, 0 and 1. In computer language these are *bits*. A sequence of eight bits in a row—for example, 01001010—is a *byte*.

The word *bit* is short for **bi**nary dig**it**. Because the computer only needs two numbers to operate, it uses a number system called base 2, or binary. Just as the number system we normally use, base 10, has ten digits (0, 1, 2, 3, 4, 5, 6, 7, 8, and 9), base 2 has two digits (0 and 1). This makes for some very long numbers; for example, in base 2 the number 45 is written 101101!

The fact that binary numbers are so vital to computer science has led to two familiar words with different meanings than you might <u>anticipate</u>. You might suppose that a kilobyte equals 1,000 bytes—after all, the prefix *kilo-* means "one thousand" in words such as *kilometer* and *kilogram*. But a kilobyte does not equal one thousand bytes; it equals 1,024 bytes. The reason for this goes back to the way the binary number system functions. Similarly, a megabyte does not equal one million bytes, even though *mega-* means "million." A megabyte is actually 1,048,576 bytes.

The next time you operate a computer, you might try looking at its basic information panel and checking the memory. It might tell you that you have 624 megabytes of available memory. So what does that really mean? How many bits can the computer store with that much memory? Now that you know about bits and bytes, you can multiply to find out. Put the number of megabytes into this equation: N × 1,048,576 × 8. If N stands for 624 megabytes, the answer is 5,234,491,392 bits. That's enough 1s and 0s, if each was only 1 millimeter wide, to more than reach across the entire United States!

Main Idea	1		
		Answer	Score
	Mark the *main idea*	M	15
	Mark the statement that is *too broad*	B	5
	Mark the statement that is *too narrow*	N	5
	a. A byte is eight bits.	☐	_____
	b. Computers run on a base two, or binary, number system.	☐	_____
	c. Number systems are interesting.	☐	_____

Subject Matter **2** This passage is mostly concerned with explaining
    ☐ a. the way the binary number system works.
    ☐ b. what base ten means.
    ☐ c. how bits and bytes work in computers.
    ☐ d. the meaning of the prefixes *kilo-* and *mega-*.   _____

Supporting Details **3** Most of the time, the prefix *kilo-* means
    ☐ a. a unit for measuring distance.
    ☐ b. one thousand.
    ☐ c. 1024.
    ☐ d. one million.   _____

Conclusion **4** You can conclude from the final paragraph that
    ☐ a. computers can store a great deal of
        information.
    ☐ b. most computers do not have enough memory.
    ☐ c. you need to be able to multiply large
        numbers to use a computer.
    ☐ d. a kilobyte is larger than a megabyte.   _____

Clarifying Devices **5** The passage discusses binary numbers in order to
    ☐ a. show that 45 can be written in two
        different ways.
    ☐ b. explain how computers operate.
    ☐ c. explain kilobytes.
    ☐ d. explain megabytes.   _____

Vocabulary in Context **6** In this passage the word <u>anticipate</u> means
    ☐ a. expect.
    ☐ b. look forward to.
    ☐ c. forget.
    ☐ d. remember.   _____

Add your scores for questions 1–6. Enter the total here   **Total**
and on the graph on page 217.   **Score**   _____

90 The Unmaking of an Anthropology Myth

Anthropologist Margaret Mead (1901–1978) said Americans could learn from the Samoans about raising children. What she had to say in her popular book *Coming of Age in Samoa* (1928) shocked people of her time. Mead, a young anthropologist in 1925–1926, studied the Samoan people. In Samoa, she said, life is free and easy. Samoa, she said, has no violence, no guilt, no anger. Samoan teens do not feel the pressures American teens feel. In Samoa, she wrote, families are large and taboos are few. Disagreements are easily settled.

Years after Mead's book was published, Australian researcher Derek Freeman disagreed. In 1983 he published *Margaret Mead and Samoa: The Making and Unmaking of an Anthropological Myth.* His own work in Samoa got very different results. He says Mead ignored facts to prove a theory. That theory proposes that culture, not biology, has the greatest influence on growing up.

Freeman also says Mead did not correctly interpret her data. He says she did not understand how the Samoans really felt toward relationships. He claims that two girls she talked to told her "stories." He says Mead was <u>duped</u> into believing these untrue stories. Also, Mead told of a Samoan life of leisure, living on the beach, without stress. Freeman said this was a fantasy. He researched Samoan crime statistics and history. The 1920s in Samoa, he says, were a time of violence.

In spite of these doubts about her first work, Mead left behind a lifetime of important contributions to the understanding of human history.

Main Idea	1	Answer	Score
	Mark the *main idea*	M	15
	Mark the statement that is *too broad*	B	5
	Mark the statement that is *too narrow*	N	5

a. Anthropological studies have been conducted in Samoa. ☐ _____

b. Derek Freeman claims that Margaret Mead's research in Samoa is incorrect. ☐ _____

c. Margaret Mead went to Samoa in 1925. ☐ _____

Subject Matter 2 This passage is mostly about
- ☐ a. Mead's work and Freeman's disagreement with it.
- ☐ b. Samoan society in the 1980s.
- ☐ c. Australian society in the 1980s.
- ☐ d. Margaret Mead's early upbringing.

_____

Supporting Details 3 Derek Freeman's book was published
- ☐ a. 20 years after Mead's book.
- ☐ b. 55 years before Mead's book.
- ☐ c. 2 to 3 years after Mead's book.
- ☐ d. 55 years after Mead's book.

_____

Conclusion 4 The final paragraph suggests that
- ☐ a. Mead spent her life studying, writing about, and contributing to anthropology.
- ☐ b. other work Mead did in her lifetime was unimportant.
- ☐ c. all of Mead's work has been questioned.
- ☐ d. Mead's research stopped with *Coming of Age in Samoa.*

_____

Clarifying Devices 5 The basic pattern used to develop this passage is
- ☐ a. personal narrative.
- ☐ b. question and answer.
- ☐ c. spatial description.
- ☐ d. statement and disagreement.

_____

Vocabulary in Context 6 The word <u>duped</u> in this passage means
- ☐ a. copied.
- ☐ b. paid.
- ☐ c. deceived or tricked.
- ☐ d. confused.

_____

Add your scores for questions 1–6. Enter the total here and on the graph on page 217.   **Total Score**

_____

91 Mexican Muralists

Brightly colored murals—huge paintings on walls or sides of buildings—brighten many cities. Murals have been around for a long time. But they became important in the Americas only in the twentieth century. One of the places they first became popular was in Mexico. And three Mexican artists became particularly well-known as muralists.

These three artists were Diego Rivera, José Orozco, and David Siqueiros. All of them had a strong political background for their works. They had lived through a civil war in the early 1900s. This war seemed to give more opportunity to poor people. The government decided to give art to those people. It wanted murals to be painted. People could see this public art and be inspired by it.

So these artists turned to murals. They covered the walls of government buildings and universities with their works. They used strong colors and huge images. Their subject matter was often the native peoples of Mexico. A mural might show people working in farm fields. Or it might show native markets and costumes. The artists' political beliefs also showed in their work. They did many paintings that presented their view of history. Often these showed the native people being crushed by the Spanish invaders.

Rivera, Orozco, and Siqueiros also painted in the United States. But sometimes their politics got them in trouble. Siqueiros painted a <u>controversial</u> mural in Los Angeles. It showed a Mexican peasant nailed to a cross. A screaming American eagle stood on top of the cross. Rivera painted a mural in Rockefeller Center in New York. It included Communist leader Lenin as an important person. Both of these murals were destroyed because certain people in power disapproved of them.

Main Idea	1			
			Answer	Score
	Mark the *main idea*		M	15
	Mark the statement that is *too broad*		B	5
	Mark the statement that is *too narrow*		N	5

a. The three great Mexican muralists expressed their political views in murals. ☐ _____

b. Murals by Siqueiros and Rivera were destroyed. ☐ _____

c. Murals are old art forms. ☐

Score 15 points for each correct answer. Score

Subject Matter   **2**   This passage is mostly concerned with
- ☐ a. Mexican politics.
- ☐ b. the murals of Rivera, Orozco, and Siqueiros.
- ☐ c. the surfaces murals are painted on.
- ☐ d. mural painting in the United States.

_____

Supporting Details   **3**   Many of the three muralists' works
- ☐ a. showed the kindness of the Spanish to the natives.
- ☐ b. were on government buildings.
- ☐ c. used complicated patterns and designs.
- ☐ d. were hated by the Mexican people.

_____

Conclusion   **4**   These muralists wanted their art to look like
- ☐ a. paintings they saw in Europe.
- ☐ b. murals that other painters were doing in the United States.
- ☐ c. something new and uniquely Mexican.
- ☐ d. something beautiful but not too serious.

_____

Clarifying Devices   **5**   The description of Siqueiros's mural in the final paragraph helps to make clear
- ☐ a. his strong painting style.
- ☐ b. his leadership in the Mexican American community.
- ☐ c. his disapproval of Mexico.
- ☐ d. his disapproval of the United States.

_____

Vocabulary in Context   **6**   In this passage <u>controversial</u> means
- ☐ a. able to stir up disagreement.
- ☐ b. able to be painted with oil paints.
- ☐ c. large.
- ☐ d. important.

_____

Add your scores for questions 1–6. Enter the total here and on the graph on page 217.   **Total Score**

_____

92 The Human Body

Human beings are recognized by such <u>external</u> body parts as the head, torso, arms, legs, and skin. On the inside, however, human beings are marvelously complex. Inside the human body are 206 bones and about 700 muscles; a brain of about 10 billion nerve cells; a small intestine about 22 feet long; a heart that beats more than 3 billion times during a lifetime; and a network of blood vessels that, if laid end to end, would encircle the earth's equator more than twice. These are just a few internal parts of the human body. What's amazing is that all parts of the human body work together. To understand how, let's start with the basics.

The human body contains about 100 trillion different *cells*. Some are bone and blood cells. Others include muscle, epithelial, and nerve cells. When similar cells group together to perform the same task, they are called *tissue*. Epithelial cells, for example, group together to form epithelial tissue. This tissue lines and protects your nose, throat, windpipe, and digestive tract. You also know this tissue as skin, which protects your body. Other tissues include blood tissue, muscle tissue, and nerve tissue.

Different tissues that work together to do a particular job are called an *organ*. Epithelial tissue, muscle tissue, blood tissue, and nerve tissue, for instance, form an organ called the *lungs*. The lungs add oxygen and remove carbon dioxide from the blood when we breathe. Other organs include the heart, stomach, liver, and intestines. Organs, tissues, and other body structures work together to form body systems. Each body system performs a special job. The nose, throat, and lungs, for example, form the respiratory system. This system controls our breathing. Other body systems include the circulatory system, digestive system, and skeletal system. When all body systems work together, the human body has life.

Main Idea 1	Answer	Score
Mark the *main idea*	M	15
Mark the statement that is *too broad*	B	5
Mark the statement that is *too narrow*	N	5
a. Humans are very complex.	☐	_____
b. The human body contains 206 bones and about 700 muscles.	☐	_____
c. The various elements of the body work together to give it life.	☐	_____

Subject Matter   **2**   The purpose of this passage is to
- ☐ a. compare the digestive and skeletal systems.
- ☐ b. describe the purpose of the small intestine.
- ☐ c. explain how the parts of the human body work together.
- ☐ d. list every part of the human body.   _____

Supporting Details   **3**   Epithelial tissue is epithelial cells that group together to
- ☐ a. line and protect your nose and throat.
- ☐ b. give the body support and movement.
- ☐ c. control breathing.
- ☐ d. remove carbon dioxide from the blood.   _____

Conclusion   **4**   After reading this passage, we can conclude that the writer has
- ☐ a. mentioned every part of the body.
- ☐ b. shown how organs are the same as tissues.
- ☐ c. mentioned some major body elements.
- ☐ d. described body elements in spatial order.   _____

Clarifying Devices   **5**   The order in which information in the passage is presented is
- ☐ a. cells, tissue, organs, body systems.
- ☐ b. cells, organs, body systems, tissue.
- ☐ c. body systems, cells, tissue, organs.
- ☐ d. cells, organs, tissue, body systems.   _____

Vocabulary in Context   **6**   In this passage the word <u>external</u> means
- ☐ a. situated on the inside of the body.
- ☐ b. seen on the outside of the body.
- ☐ c. something that is not significant.
- ☐ d. an outside force.   _____

Add your scores for questions 1–6. Enter the total here and on the graph on page 217.   **Total Score**   _____

93 Shapes That Cover

Probably somewhere in your home you have a floor or wall covered with square tiles. The majority of homes have a tile pattern somewhere, usually in kitchens and bathrooms. Have you ever thought about the geometry of tiled surfaces? Why are squares used so often? Can other geometric shapes such as triangles and circles be used equally well?

It turns out that not all shapes can be used to completely cover a flat surface. Such a covering has the mathematical name of *tessellation*. A tessellation is a complete covering with no holes and no overlaps. Squares will tessellate a surface, but circles won't. Another shape that works is a regular hexagon. This six-sided shape is seen in floor tiles as well as in such materials as chicken wire.

Another familiar tessellation is one made from rectangular bricks that are about 4 inches long and 8 inches wide. Why does this shape work well to cover a surface? This rectangle is actually two squares put together. Any rectangle twice as long as it is wide will work for this tessellation. The diagram shows one possible arrangement. If you take a pencil and divide each rectangle into two squares, you'll see the square grid that <u>underlies</u> the tiling.

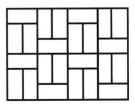

Once you starting looking for tessellation patterns, you will observe them in many places. You might keep a sketchbook of the possibilities you notice in walls, brick paths, and floors. Then, the next time you are planning to tile a floor or wall, you'll have choices other than plain old boring squares!

Main Idea 1 ——————————————————————————

	Answer	Score
Mark the *main idea*	M	15
Mark the statement that is *too broad*	B	5
Mark the statement that is *too narrow*	N	5

a. Geometry helps to cover floors. ☐ _____

b. Various geometric shapes can be used to cover a floor or wall. ☐ _____

c. Squares and hexagons will tesselate a surface. ☐ _____

Subject Matter　2　This passage is mainly about
- [ ] a. rectangles twice as long as they are wide.
- [ ] b. different kinds of tile patterns that will completely cover a surface.
- [ ] c. how to choose a type of floor for a kitchen or bathroom.
- [ ] d. floor coverings using six-sided pieces.

　　_____

Supporting Details　3　One geometric shape that *cannot* be used in a tessellation is the
- [ ] a. square.
- [ ] b. rectangle.
- [ ] c. circle.
- [ ] d. hexagon.

　　_____

Conclusion　4　It is reasonable to conclude that
- [ ] a. squares and rectangles are often used in tessellations.
- [ ] b. rectangular tiles cost more than square tiles.
- [ ] c. a hexagon is a five-sided figure.
- [ ] d. it is hard to lay out a floor with a tesselation.

　　_____

Clarifying Devices　5　The writer explains tessellations through
- [ ] a. descriptions and a diagram.
- [ ] b. comparisons and instructions.
- [ ] c. formulas and procedures.
- [ ] d. explaining how to draw them.

　　_____

Vocabulary in Context　6　In this passage the word underlies means
- [ ] a. keeps the pieces separated.
- [ ] b. rests comfortably.
- [ ] c. forms the foundation of.
- [ ] d. is used as a glue.

　　_____

Add your scores for questions 1–6. Enter the total here and on the graph on page 217.　　Total Score

　_____

94 Chinese Waterways

China has many natural barriers, including <u>vast</u> mountains, deserts, and oceans that separate its regions. These natural barriers make travel and communication difficult, but from earliest times people have taken advantage of the rivers. Farmers who lived inland used the rivers as roads. They sent their crops on boats to ocean ports. The rivers also provided water for people, animals, and crops. The sandy soil along the banks of the rivers gave them good farmland.

The Chang, or Yangtze, is China's longest river. It is the third longest river in the world. Many cities along the Chang River are important river ports. This river handles about 80 percent of China's inland water traffic. The Chang River is a main waterway connecting eastern and western China.

The Huang, or Yellow, is China's second longest river. It is the fifth longest river in the world. Its brownish-yellow water gave it its name. Before 1949, the Huang River often flooded, causing damage. Now, after 40 years of building river controls, such as dikes, the Huang is more predictable.

China's Grand Canal is the world's oldest and longest man-made waterway. It is more than 1,000 miles long. The canal was begun in the sixth century B.C. It was completed in the 13th century A.D. The Grand Canal links several rivers, including the Chang and the Huang. Before railroads were built, it served as the main method of travel between northern and southern China.

The canal, like China's rivers, is still in use today. China's waterways continue to carry goods and people. They help connect China's vast regions. In many ways, they are China's lifelines.

Main Idea	1	Answer	Score
	Mark the *main idea*	M	15
	Mark the statement that is *too broad*	B	5
	Mark the statement that is *too narrow*	N	5

a.	Waterways are important to Chinese life.	☐ _____
b.	Goods are transported on the Grand Canal.	☐ _____
c.	Rivers help countries to develop.	☐ _____

Subject Matter **2** Another good title for this passage would be

☐ a. Two Chinese Rivers.

☐ b. A Short History of China.

☐ c. A Transportation System Built on Water.

☐ d. The Importance of the Grand Canal.   _____

Supporting Details **3** China's longest river is the

☐ a. Chang.

☐ b. Yellow.

☐ c. Grand.

☐ d. Huang.   _____

Conclusion **4** In earlier times, living very close to the Huang River was

☐ a. smart.

☐ b. required if you were a trader.

☐ c. done only by the very old.

☐ d. dangerous.   _____

Clarifying Devices **5** The rivers are called *lifelines* in the final paragraph because

☐ a. they are places where people can fish.

☐ b. boats on them are pulled by ropes.

☐ c. they provide vital communication and transport services.

☐ d. they are long and narrow.   _____

Vocabulary in Context **6** The word <u>vast</u> means

☐ a. quick.

☐ b. huge.

☐ c. changing.

☐ d. worthless.   _____

Add your scores for questions 1–6. Enter the total here and on the graph on page 217.   Total
Score   _____

95 Singing the Blues

What do you know about the music called "the blues"? Do you think it is the same thing as jazz? Well, in some ways the two types of music are related, but the blues has its own history and development that is quite distinct from that of jazz.

The beginnings of the blues date back to the nineteenth century. After the Civil War, when the slaves were freed in the South, life was hard. As African Americans banded together into their own communities, the blues began to develop out of some of their earlier music. Songs were generally not written down, and they usually expressed their composers' feelings. Many were about the difficult times, natural disasters, alcohol, the effects of crime, and the loss of loved ones.

Some people say Mississippi was the birthplace of the blues, but early blues singers were also found in Texas, Alabama, and several other Southern states. As time passed, the blues moved north. Chicago became an important blues center.

What does the blues sound like? Stringed instruments, especially the guitar, are important in blues playing. A piano is also often used. Piano players frequently get the sound they want by "crushing" the keys, or playing two notes not quite at the same time. Many blues songs are built around a pattern of three grouped lines. The first two lines are repeated ("My man has left me, and I'm feeling so blue"), and then the third line is a sort of comment ("Don't know what I'll do if he don't come back soon").

Who were some legendary blues figures? Bessie Smith was an early female singer; Robert Johnson became famous for his throbbing, whining guitar. Later blues greats such as Muddy Waters had a direct influence on such groups as the Rolling Stones—in fact, until his death the Stones visited Muddy Waters whenever they played Chicago.

Main Idea	1		
		Answer	Score
	Mark the *main idea*	M	15
	Mark the statement that is *too broad*	B	5
	Mark the statement that is *too narrow*	N	5

a. The blues has an interesting history and development. ☐ _____

b. The blues influenced the Rolling Stones. ☐ _____

c. The blues is a kind of American music. ☐ _____

Score 15 points for each correct answer.   **Score**

Subject Matter   2   This passage is mostly about
- [ ] a. how the blues and jazz are similar.
- [ ] b. the development of the blues.
- [ ] c. Robert Johnson and Muddy Waters.
- [ ] d. the birthplace of the blues.

_____

Supporting Details   3   An instrument commonly used in blues playing is the
- [ ] a. trumpet.
- [ ] b. drum.
- [ ] c. guitar.
- [ ] d. xylophone.

_____

Conclusion   4   Based on information from this passage, the blues seems to have had the most effect on
- [ ] a. rap.
- [ ] b. rock and roll.
- [ ] c. the tango.
- [ ] d. classical music.

_____

Clarifying Devices   5   One device that the writer of this passage uses to organize ideas is
- [ ] a. diagrams.
- [ ] b. questions.
- [ ] c. spatial descriptions.
- [ ] d. song lyrics.

_____

Vocabulary in Context   6   In this passage the word <u>legendary</u> means
- [ ] a. untrue.
- [ ] b. very famous.
- [ ] c. very loud.
- [ ] d. large.

_____

Add your scores for questions 1–6. Enter the total here   **Total**
and on the graph on page 217.   **Score**

_____

96 Animal Behavior

Ants release scent spots to guide them through mazes. Honeybees recognize landmarks to find their way home. Groundhogs hibernate to survive cold winters. All of these are examples of animal behavior.

Behavior is the response of an organism to the things around it. Some behavior is a response to an external, or outside, stimulus in the environment. A mouse, for example, runs when it sees a cat. The running is the response to the external stimulus of the cat. Other behavior is a response to an <u>internal</u> stimulus. An example is a hungry cat chasing a mouse. The chasing is the response to the internal stimulus of hunger.

There are two types of behavior: innate and learned. *Innate behavior* is an automatic, inherited response. Reflexes and instincts are both innate behaviors. A *reflex* is a direct, immediate response to a stimulus. A reflex, for example, enables a cat to land on its feet most of the time. An *instinct* is a series of actions in response to a stimulus. An instinct, for instance, enables a newborn mammal to find and feed from its mother's breast. Other instincts are animal migration, mating, and hibernation.

Learned behavior is behavior that changes due to experience. One way it may be learned is through trial and error. A bird building its first nest, for example, collects a variety of materials including twigs, plastic, and paper. The bird soon learns that only twigs make a sturdy nest. Eventually, the bird modifies its behavior and collects only twigs. Behavior also may be learned from association with a stimulus. An example is people standing at a pond throwing bread crumbs into it. Fish in the pond see the people and then the food. The fish come to the surface and eat. The fish eventually associate the stimulus of people with food. The fish respond by coming to the surface whenever people are there, even if they don't toss bread crumbs.

Main Idea 1

	Answer	Score
Mark the *main idea*	M	15
Mark the statement that is *too broad*	B	5
Mark the statement that is *too narrow*	N	5

a. All animals have behaviors.	☐	_____
b. Behavior is the response of an organism to the things around it.	☐	_____
c. Some behaviors are learned by trial and error.	☐	_____

Subject Matter   **2**   The purpose of this passage is to

☐ a. explain types of animal behavior.

☐ b. explain what an instinct is.

☐ c. describe animal hibernation.

☐ d. give an example of trial and error learning.   _____

Supporting Details   **3**   Animal migration is an example of

☐ a. an instinct.

☐ b. trial and error.

☐ c. an external stimulus.

☐ d. a learned behavior.   _____

Conclusion   **4**   An external stimulus might cause you as a human to

☐ a. eat when you are hungry.

☐ b. laugh when you hear a funny joke.

☐ c. sleep when you are tired.

☐ d. drink water when you are thirsty.   _____

Clarifying Devices   **5**   To help the reader understand the terms in this passage, the author presents

☐ a. arguments and opinions.

☐ b. definitions and examples.

☐ c. comparisons and contrasts.

☐ d. scientific experiments and studies.   _____

Vocabulary in Context   **6**   In this passage the word <u>internal</u> means

☐ a. above.

☐ b. below.

☐ c. outside.

☐ d. inside.   _____

Add your scores for questions 1–6. Enter the total here and on the graph on page 217.   **Total Score**   _____

97 Using Exchange Rates

Are you—or is someone you know—planning a trip outside the United States? If so, it may be necessary to use math skills when making purchases. Each country has a different form of money, and a traveler will want to know how much a product or meal costs in U.S. dollars.

To convert foreign money, a traveler needs to know the current exchange rate. This is a number that helps a person figure out how the foreign <u>currency</u> translates into dollars. Exchange rates for foreign currencies change all the time. They depend on how much a nation's money is in demand by other nations. Currency values were once based on the value of gold, but now they are set by international agreements.

Exchange rates are found in the business sections of most newspapers. For example, currency in Denmark is called *kroner.* You might find that one dollar currently equals 6.61 Danish kroner. To change dollars to kroner, multiply by 6.61. To change kroner to dollars, divide by 6.61. Since doing this type of arithmetic in a crowded souvenir shop, even with a calculator, might be difficult, many people use a conversion table. Before you leave on your trip, make a table like the one shown below. You can use your table to estimate the dollar amount of an item you'd like to buy. For example, an item marked as 130 kroner will cost between $15 and $20. Doing a little practice ahead of time can help you stick to your travel budget. Being prepared may also prevent unpleasant surprises when your charge card bill arrives!

Dollars	Kroner	Dollars	Kroner	Dollars	Kroner	Dollars	Kroner
$1	6.61	$15	99.15	$40	264.40	$70	462.70
$2	13.22	$20	132.20	$45	297.45	$80	528.80
$5	33.05	$25	165.25	$50	330.50	$90	594.90
$10	66.10	$30	198.30	$60	396.60	$100	661.00

Main Idea

1

	Answer	Score
Mark the *main idea*	**M**	15
Mark the statement that is *too broad*	**B**	5
Mark the statement that is *too narrow*	**N**	5

a. Exchange rates can be used to convert one country's money into another's. ☐ ___

b. Exchange rates are set by international agreements. ☐ ___

c. Some travel requires different forms of money. ☐ ___

Subject Matter　**2**　This passage is mainly concerned with
　　　　　　　□ a. comparing U.S. and Danish money.
　　　　　　　□ b. spending money when traveling outside
　　　　　　　　　 the United States.
　　　　　　　□ c. how money values are decided on.
　　　　　　　□ d. estimating prices when traveling outside
　　　　　　　　　 the United States.　　　　　　　_____

Supporting　　**3**　Exchange rates for foreign monies
Details　　　　　 □ a. never change.
　　　　　　　□ b. change frequently.
　　　　　　　□ c. can only be found in travel guidebooks.
　　　　　　　□ d. are always given in kroner.　　　　_____

Conclusion　　**4**　Based on information in this passage, it is
　　　　　　　reasonable to conclude that German money
　　　　　　　□ a. has a value that changes often.
　　　　　　　□ b. has the same exchange rate as Danish money.
　　　　　　　□ c. cannot be converted into American money.
　　　　　　　□ d. has a value that keeps going up.　　_____

Clarifying　　**5**　The table in the passage is intended as a help for
Devices　　　　 □ a. buying inexpensive souvenirs.
　　　　　　　□ b. figuring out the price of an item when it is
　　　　　　　　　 given in Danish kroner.
　　　　　　　□ c. figuring out distances in Denmark.
　　　　　　　□ d. bargaining down a price in Denmark.　_____

Vocabulary　　**6**　In this passage the word <u>currency</u> means
in Context　　　 □ a. exchange.
　　　　　　　□ b. money.
　　　　　　　□ c. expensive.
　　　　　　　□ d. cents.　　　　　　　　　　_____

Add your scores for questions 1–6. Enter the total here　**Total**
and on the graph on page 217.　　　　　　　　**Score**　_____

98 Fewer Births, Longer Lives

Population change depends mainly on a country's birth and death rates. These rates are expressed as the number of births and deaths for every 1,000 people in a year. The difference between the birth rate and the death rate gives the natural increase or decrease of population.

Take the case of Italy, whose population today is about 57¹/₂ million. The population increased slowly during most of the twentieth century. By 1996, though, the increase had almost stopped. Italy now has a birth rate of 10 per thousand and a death rate of 10 per thousand, so the natural change is zero. Italy has zero population growth.

Italy's lower death rate is mainly because of better medical care. Fewer babies die and people now live longer. The average life expectancy in Italy is age 75 for males and age 81 for females.

Italy's lower birth rate has several causes. One is that in the 1970s an increase in unemployment left people feeling financially insecure. They chose to have fewer children. Another is that more people moved from rural to urban areas. Living and raising children in the city was more costly, so people had fewer children. A third reason is that more women now have careers outside of the home. They choose to have fewer children. And many more children now live at home until they are about 30 years old. They marry later and might not have children at all. Finally, many adults want a lifestyle that is not <u>compatible</u> with raising big families.

There is speculation that Italy's growth rate will be less than zero and that the total population will start to decline. It is possible that in 100 years' time there will only be 19 million people living in Italy.

Main Idea   **1**

	Answer	Score
Mark the *main idea*	M	15
Mark the statement that is *too broad*	B	5
Mark the statement that is *too narrow*	N	5

a. Populations may increase or decrease. ☐ _____

b. Italy has achieved zero population growth for a variety of reasons. ☐ _____

c. Italy has a birth rate of 10 per thousand. ☐ _____

Score 15 points for each correct answer.   Score

Subject Matter   2   This passage is mostly about
    ☐ a. what zero population growth means.
    ☐ b. why many Italian women work.
    ☐ c. what Italy's population will be in the future.
    ☐ d. why Italy has zero population growth. _____

Supporting Details   3   The yearly death rate in Italy is
    ☐ a. zero.
    ☐ b. 10 per 1,000.
    ☐ c. $57\frac{1}{2}$ million.
    ☐ d. 1,000 a year. _____

Conclusion   4   The passage shows that there is no one single reason for
    ☐ a. Italy's lower death rate.
    ☐ b. Italy's lower birth rate.
    ☐ c. Italy's present employment situation.
    ☐ d. the policies of Italy's government. _____

Clarifying Devices   5   Information about Italy's birth rate is made clearer by the use of
    ☐ a. long sentences.
    ☐ b. stories about women in the workplace.
    ☐ c. transitional words and phrases.
    ☐ d. a bulleted list. _____

Vocabulary in Context   6   The word <u>compatible</u> means
    ☐ a. in agreement.
    ☐ b. understandable.
    ☐ c. legal.
    ☐ d. valued. _____

Add your scores for questions 1–6. Enter the total here and on the graph on page 217.   Total Score _____

99 A Controversial Novel

The Catcher in the Rye by J. D. Salinger was published more than 50 years ago. The novel deals with a common topic—a confused young teenager trying to make sense of the world around him. And yet even today it is one of the most frequently banned books in American schools.

Why has this book caused such a furor? It helps to think back to the times when it was published. The year was 1951, and the American public was very conservative. <u>Profanity</u> and open discussion of sexual issues did not occur that frequently in adult novels. They *never* came up in books of interest to younger readers.

And yet both were important elements of *The Catcher in the Rye.* The book's young hero, Holden Caulfield, tells his memories of four days in his life, just after he has been expelled from school. His speech includes a fair amount of swearing. He also wishes for sexual experiences, though he never actually has any. He has so much trouble with the "phoniness" he perceives all around him that he ends up in a mental hospital.

The novel was hailed as a great work when it was first published. College students in particular identified with it, seeing many of their own views of the world in Holden's. But it has never overcome its reputation as a shocking story. Many high schools still refuse to teach it, even though their students have probably read much more offensive works.

Though Salinger wrote a number of short stories, *The Catcher in the Rye* is his only novel. He has chosen to live in isolation in New Hampshire for many years, refusing to submit to interviews.

Main Idea 1

	Answer	Score
Mark the *main idea*	M	15
Mark the statement that is *too broad*	B	5
Mark the statement that is *too narrow*	N	5

a. J. D. Salinger wrote *The Catcher in the Rye.* ☐ _____

b. *The Catcher in the Rye,* the story of a young teen, is a controversial novel. ☐ _____

c. The main character in *The Catcher in the Rye* does a lot of swearing. ☐ _____

Subject Matter 2 This passage is mainly about
- [ ] a. the writings of J. D. Salinger.
- [ ] b. how *The Catcher in the Rye* offended people.
- [ ] c. an analysis of Holden Caulfield's family life.
- [ ] d. novels of the 1950s.   _____

Supporting Details 3 Holden Caulfield's story takes place
- [ ] a. in his dormitory at school.
- [ ] b. when he is about 21 years old.
- [ ] c. just after he is expelled from school.
- [ ] d. in the summer, just before school starts.   _____

Conclusion 4 We can conclude from this passage that J. D. Salinger
- [ ] a. knows little about how teenagers think.
- [ ] b. continues to write constantly.
- [ ] c. is only an average novelist.
- [ ] d. does not like to discuss his writings in public.   _____

Clarifying Devices 5 The quotation marks around "phoniness" in the third paragraph suggest that
- [ ] a. it is a direct quote from the novel.
- [ ] b. it is a word the writer of the passage disapproves of.
- [ ] c. Holden never said it.
- [ ] d. the writer thinks it is spelled wrong.   _____

Vocabulary in Context 6 <u>Profanity</u> means
- [ ] a. anger.
- [ ] b. confusion.
- [ ] c. sex.
- [ ] d. swearing.   _____

Add your scores for questions 1–6. Enter the total here and on the graph on page 217. **Total Score** _____

100 Why Equations Don't Have Answers

If you are like most people, your earliest experiences in mathematics were computing answers to arithmetic problems. Many students have difficulty when they first begin studying algebra because they have the belief that *all of* math is about determining answers. To understand why this is untrue, compare these mathematical problems:

What is 45×678? $45 \times 678 = n$

The first problem is a question and it has an answer: 30,510. The second problem is not a question; rather, it is a statement in the form of an equation. To make this statement true, you need to find a number value for the letter n so that both sides of the equation are equal. Of course, the correct value is the same as the answer to the question "What is 45×678?"—30,510. This value, 30,510, is called the *solution* to the equation—a number that makes both sides of the equation equal.

Why is this distinction between answer and solution important for students to understand? Most equations are much more complicated than $45 \times 678 = n$. In the more complicated ones, performing a series of steps is necessary to arrive at the solution. To do this correctly, students learn they must "do the same thing" to both sides of an equation at each step. Solving a complicated equation involves working through a whole series of equations till you end up with a simple one like $n = 30{,}510$.

Many equations do not have a single number for a solution; instead, they have a whole set of numbers. In the equation $2a \times b = 12$, for example, one solution is to substitute 2 for a and 3 for b, but another is to substitute 1 and 6 (try it). And infinitely many more solutions exist. So "What is the answer to $2a \times b = 12$?" is a meaningless question. There is no answer to such an equation, only a set of solutions.

Main Idea	1			
			Answer	**Score**
	Mark the *main idea*		M	15
	Mark the statement that is *too broad*		B	5
	Mark the statement that is *too narrow*		N	5

a. Some equations involve going through a whole series of steps. ☐ _____

b. Arithmetic and algebra are different. ☐ _____

c. Equations can't be "answered"; they must be "solved." ☐ _____

Subject Matter   **2**   This passage is mainly about
☐ a. doing arithmetic accurately.
☐ b. why equations have solutions rather than answers.
☐ c. what *n* stands for in two different problems.
☐ d. solving difficult equations.   _____

Supporting Details   **3**   At each step in solving an equation, you must
☐ a. check that you have the right answer.
☐ b. show your solution on a graph.
☐ c. show your solution on a diagram
☐ d. do the same thing to both sides.   _____

Conclusion   **4**   The author has written this passage because
☐ a. some students find arithmetic confusing.
☐ b. some students find algebra confusing.
☐ c. some equations have many answers.
☐ d. all equations are quite complicated.   _____

Clarifying Devices   **5**   The passage explains the distinction between *answer* and *solution* by
☐ a. presenting a diagram.
☐ b. giving and explaining examples.
☐ c. showing the solution to a difficult equation.
☐ d. describing a graph.   _____

Vocabulary in Context   **6**   In this passage the word <u>meaningless</u> means
☐ a. having several meanings.
☐ b. being very important.
☐ c. without meaning.
☐ d. meaning different things at different times.   _____

Add your scores for questions 1–6. Enter the total here and on the graph on page 217.   **Total Score**   _____

Answer Keys

Answer Key: Passages 1–25

Passage 1:	1a. **M**	1b. **B**	1c. **N**	2. **a**	3. **d**	4. **c**	5. **d**	6. **a**
Passage 2:	1a. **N**	1b. **M**	1c. **B**	2. **b**	3. **a**	4. **c**	5. **b**	6. **d**
Passage 3:	1a. **N**	1b. **M**	1c. **B**	2. **b**	3. **d**	4. **b**	5. **a**	6. **b**
Passage 4:	1a. **N**	1b. **M**	1c. **B**	2. **d**	3. **a**	4. **b**	5. **a**	6. **d**
Passage 5:	1a. **M**	1b. **N**	1c. **B**	2. **a**	3. **b**	4. **d**	5. **a**	6. **c**
Passage 6:	1a. **M**	1b. **B**	1c. **N**	2. **c**	3. **d**	4. **b**	5. **d**	6. **c**
Passage 7:	1a. **B**	1b. **M**	1c. **N**	2. **d**	3. **b**	4. **c**	5. **a**	6. **a**
Passage 8:	1a. **B**	1b. **M**	1c. **N**	2. **a**	3. **c**	4. **b**	5. **d**	6. **a**
Passage 9:	1a. **N**	1b. **B**	1c. **M**	2. **b**	3. **c**	4. **a**	5. **c**	6. **a**
Passage 10:	1a. **B**	1b. **M**	1c. **N**	2. **c**	3. **b**	4. **c**	5. **a**	6. **d**
Passage 11:	1a. **N**	1b. **B**	1c. **M**	2. **a**	3. **b**	4. **b**	5. **b**	6. **c**
Passage 12:	1a. **N**	1b. **M**	1c. **B**	2. **c**	3. **b**	4. **a**	5. **c**	6. **b**
Passage 13:	1a. **M**	1b. **N**	1c. **B**	2. **b**	3. **d**	4. **a**	5. **a**	6. **c**
Passage 14:	1a. **N**	1b. **B**	1c. **M**	2. **c**	3. **a**	4. **b**	5. **d**	6. **d**
Passage 15:	1a. **B**	1b. **M**	1c. **N**	2. **c**	3. **a**	4. **b**	5. **b**	6. **d**
Passage 16:	1a. **M**	1b. **N**	1c. **B**	2. **d**	3. **c**	4. **a**	5. **b**	6. **a**
Passage 17:	1a. **N**	1b. **M**	1c. **B**	2. **a**	3. **c**	4. **d**	5. **b**	6. **b**
Passage 18:	1a. **B**	1b. **N**	1c. **M**	2. **c**	3. **d**	4. **b**	5. **b**	6. **a**
Passage 19:	1a. **M**	1b. **B**	1c. **N**	2. **c**	3. **b**	4. **b**	5. **d**	6. **a**
Passage 20:	1a. **M**	1b. **B**	1c. **N**	2. **c**	3. **d**	4. **b**	5. **a**	6. **d**
Passage 21:	1a. **N**	1b. **B**	1c. **M**	2. **c**	3. **a**	4. **b**	5. **b**	6. **d**
Passage 22:	1a. **B**	1b. **N**	1c. **M**	2. **b**	3. **c**	4. **d**	5. **a**	6. **b**
Passage 23:	1a. **N**	1b. **B**	1c. **M**	2. **c**	3. **b**	4. **d**	5. **b**	6. **c**
Passage 24:	1a. **N**	1b. **B**	1c. **M**	2. **c**	3. **a**	4. **b**	5. **b**	6. **a**
Passage 25:	1a. **N**	1b. **M**	1c. **B**	2. **c**	3. **c**	4. **c**	5. **d**	6. **c**

Answer Key: Passages 26–50

Passage 26:	1a. **M**	1b. **N**	1c. **B**	2. **b**	3. **d**	4. **b**	5. **c**	6. **c**
Passage 27:	1a. **N**	1b. **M**	1c. **B**	2. **d**	3. **c**	4. **a**	5. **b**	6. **c**
Passage 28:	1a. **B**	1b. **M**	1c. **N**	2. **a**	3. **d**	4. **a**	5. **b**	6. **c**
Passage 29:	1a. **M**	1b. **N**	1c. **B**	2. **b**	3. **d**	4. **a**	5. **c**	6. **b**
Passage 30:	1a. **M**	1b. **N**	1c. **B**	2. **c**	3. **d**	4. **d**	5. **a**	6. **a**
Passage 31:	1a. **B**	1b. **N**	1c. **M**	2. **d**	3. **a**	4. **a**	5. **c**	6. **b**
Passage 32:	1a. **B**	1b. **M**	1c. **N**	2. **c**	3. **c**	4. **b**	5. **a**	6. **d**
Passage 33:	1a. **M**	1b. **B**	1c. **N**	2. **c**	3. **b**	4. **a**	5. **a**	6. **d**
Passage 34:	1a. **B**	1b. **N**	1c. **M**	2. **a**	3. **c**	4. **c**	5. **b**	6. **d**
Passage 35:	1a. **B**	1b. **N**	1c. **M**	2. **b**	3. **a**	4. **d**	5. **c**	6. **b**
Passage 36:	1a. **M**	1b. **B**	1c. **N**	2. **d**	3. **b**	4. **d**	5. **a**	6. **a**
Passage 37:	1a. **N**	1b. **B**	1c. **M**	2. **b**	3. **c**	4. **c**	5. **a**	6. **b**
Passage 38:	1a. **M**	1b. **B**	1c. **N**	2. **c**	3. **a**	4. **a**	5. **b**	6. **c**
Passage 39:	1a. **M**	1b. **B**	1c. **N**	2. **a**	3. **c**	4. **d**	5. **c**	6. **b**
Passage 40:	1a. **N**	1b. **B**	1c. **M**	2. **a**	3. **b**	4. **d**	5. **a**	6. **b**
Passage 41:	1a. **M**	1b. **N**	1c. **B**	2. **b**	3. **b**	4. **b**	5. **c**	6. **d**
Passage 42:	1a. **M**	1b. **N**	1c. **B**	2. **d**	3. **b**	4. **a**	5. **c**	6. **a**
Passage 43:	1a. **N**	1b. **B**	1c. **M**	2. **a**	3. **c**	4. **d**	5. **c**	6. **b**
Passage 44:	1a. **M**	1b. **N**	1c. **B**	2. **b**	3. **a**	4. **c**	5. **d**	6. **b**
Passage 45:	1a. **N**	1b. **M**	1c. **B**	2. **c**	3. **b**	4. **c**	5. **d**	6. **a**
Passage 46:	1a. **N**	1b. **B**	1c. **M**	2. **b**	3. **d**	4. **a**	5. **a**	6. **a**
Passage 47:	1a. **N**	1b. **B**	1c. **M**	2. **a**	3. **d**	4. **b**	5. **b**	6. **a**
Passage 48:	1a. **M**	1b. **B**	1c. **N**	2. **b**	3. **d**	4. **d**	5. **b**	6. **c**
Passage 49:	1a. **M**	1b. **B**	1c. **N**	2. **b**	3. **d**	4. **c**	5. **a**	6. **b**
Passage 50:	1a. **M**	1b. **N**	1c. **B**	2. **b**	3. **c**	4. **b**	5. **a**	6. **c**

Answer Key: Passages 51–75

Passage 51:	1a. **M**	1b. **B**	1c. **N**	2. **d**	3. **a**	4. **b**	5. **c**	6. **a**
Passage 52:	1a. **B**	1b. **M**	1c. **N**	2. **b**	3. **c**	4. **b**	5. **d**	6. **c**
Passage 53:	1a. **M**	1b. **N**	1c. **B**	2. **a**	3. **d**	4. **b**	5. **c**	6. **d**
Passage 54:	1a. **N**	1b. **B**	1c. **M**	2. **b**	3. **c**	4. **d**	5. **a**	6. **c**
Passage 55:	1a. **N**	1b. **B**	1c. **M**	2. **b**	3. **d**	4. **a**	5. **c**	6. **b**
Passage 56:	1a. **B**	1b. **M**	1c. **N**	2. **a**	3. **d**	4. **b**	5. **a**	6. **a**
Passage 57:	1a. **M**	1b. **B**	1c. **N**	2. **c**	3. **d**	4. **a**	5. **b**	6. **a**
Passage 58:	1a. **M**	1b. **N**	1c. **B**	2. **b**	3. **c**	4. **d**	5. **c**	6. **a**
Passage 59:	1a. **M**	1b. **N**	1c. **B**	2. **c**	3. **d**	4. **a**	5. **c**	6. **a**
Passage 60:	1a. **M**	1b. **N**	1c. **B**	2. **c**	3. **b**	4. **c**	5. **a**	6. **a**
Passage 61:	1a. **N**	1b. **M**	1c. **B**	2. **c**	3. **b**	4. **d**	5. **d**	6. **a**
Passage 62:	1a. **N**	1b. **B**	1c. **M**	2. **a**	3. **d**	4. **b**	5. **b**	6. **c**
Passage 63:	1a. **M**	1b. **B**	1c. **N**	2. **a**	3. **c**	4. **b**	5. **c**	6. **b**
Passage 64:	1a. **B**	1b. **N**	1c. **M**	2. **b**	3. **a**	4. **c**	5. **d**	6. **d**
Passage 65:	1a. **N**	1b. **M**	1c. **B**	2. **d**	3. **b**	4. **d**	5. **c**	6. **a**
Passage 66:	1a. **N**	1b. **B**	1c. **M**	2. **b**	3. **d**	4. **a**	5. **c**	6. **b**
Passage 67:	1a. **B**	1b. **M**	1c. **N**	2. **b**	3. **d**	4. **a**	5. **b**	6. **c**
Passage 68:	1a. **B**	1b. **M**	1c. **N**	2. **a**	3. **c**	4. **d**	5. **b**	6. **b**
Passage 69:	1a. **B**	1b. **M**	1c. **N**	2. **b**	3. **b**	4. **b**	5. **c**	6. **d**
Passage 70:	1a. **M**	1b. **B**	1c. **N**	2. **b**	3. **d**	4. **d**	5. **d**	6. **a**
Passage 71:	1a. **N**	1b. **M**	1c. **B**	2. **a**	3. **c**	4. **d**	5. **b**	6. **b**
Passage 72:	1a. **B**	1b. **N**	1c. **M**	2. **c**	3. **a**	4. **b**	5. **d**	6. **a**
Passage 73:	1a. **B**	1b. **N**	1c. **M**	2. **d**	3. **b**	4. **c**	5. **a**	6. **c**
Passage 74:	1a. **M**	1b. **N**	1c. **B**	2. **b**	3. **d**	4. **c**	5. **a**	6. **b**
Passage 75:	1a. **M**	1b. **N**	1c. **B**	2. **b**	3. **d**	4. **d**	5. **a**	6. **b**

Answer Key: Passages 76–100

Passage 76:	1a. **B**	1b. **N**	1c. **M**	2. **c**	3. **b**	4. **d**	5. **b**	6. **b**
Passage 77:	1a. **N**	1b. **M**	1c. **B**	2. **a**	3. **c**	4. **a**	5. **b**	6. **c**
Passage 78:	1a. **M**	1b. **N**	1c. **B**	2. **c**	3. **d**	4. **b**	5. **a**	6. **c**
Passage 79:	1a. **B**	1b. **M**	1c. **N**	2. **d**	3. **b**	4. **a**	5. **b**	6. **d**
Passage 80:	1a. **N**	1b. **B**	1c. **M**	2. **c**	3. **d**	4. **a**	5. **c**	6. **a**
Passage 81:	1a. **B**	1b. **N**	1c. **M**	2. **b**	3. **d**	4. **b**	5. **b**	6. **c**
Passage 82:	1a. **B**	1b. **M**	1c. **N**	2. **c**	3. **b**	4. **b**	5. **c**	6. **a**
Passage 83:	1a. **B**	1b. **M**	1c. **N**	2. **a**	3. **b**	4. **d**	5. **a**	6. **c**
Passage 84:	1a. **B**	1b. **N**	1c. **M**	2. **b**	3. **a**	4. **d**	5. **a**	6. **c**
Passage 85:	1a. **N**	1b. **B**	1c. **M**	2. **b**	3. **d**	4. **c**	5. **a**	6. **c**
Passage 86:	1a. **M**	1b. **N**	1c. **B**	2. **a**	3. **c**	4. **d**	5. **c**	6. **b**
Passage 87:	1a. **B**	1b. **M**	1c. **N**	2. **b**	3. **d**	4. **d**	5. **c**	6. **a**
Passage 88:	1a. **M**	1b. **N**	1c. **B**	2. **d**	3. **b**	4. **c**	5. **a**	6. **d**
Passage 89:	1a. **N**	1b. **M**	1c. **B**	2. **c**	3. **b**	4. **a**	5. **b**	6. **a**
Passage 90:	1a. **B**	1b. **M**	1c. **N**	2. **a**	3. **d**	4. **a**	5. **d**	6. **c**
Passage 91:	1a. **M**	1b. **N**	1c. **B**	2. **b**	3. **b**	4. **c**	5. **d**	6. **a**
Passage 92:	1a. **B**	1b. **N**	1c. **M**	2. **c**	3. **a**	4. **c**	5. **a**	6. **b**
Passage 93:	1a. **B**	1b. **M**	1c. **N**	2. **b**	3. **c**	4. **a**	5. **a**	6. **c**
Passage 94:	1a. **M**	1b. **N**	1c. **B**	2. **c**	3. **a**	4. **d**	5. **c**	6. **b**
Passage 95:	1a. **M**	1b. **N**	1c. **B**	2. **b**	3. **c**	4. **b**	5. **b**	6. **b**
Passage 96:	1a. **B**	1b. **M**	1c. **N**	2. **a**	3. **a**	4. **b**	5. **b**	6. **d**
Passage 97:	1a. **M**	1b. **N**	1c. **B**	2. **d**	3. **b**	4. **a**	5. **b**	6. **b**
Passage 98:	1a. **B**	1b. **M**	1c. **N**	2. **d**	3. **b**	4. **b**	5. **c**	6. **a**
Passage 99:	1a. **B**	1b. **M**	1c. **N**	2. **b**	3. **c**	4. **d**	5. **a**	6. **d**
Passage 100:	1a. **N**	1b. **B**	1c. **M**	2. **b**	3. **d**	4. **b**	5. **b**	6. **c**

Diagnostic Charts
For Student Correction

Diagnostic Chart: Passages 1–25

Directions: For each passage, write your answers to the left of the dotted line in the blocks for each skill category. Then correct your answers using the Answer Key on page 204. If your answer is correct, do not make any more marks in the block. If your answer is incorrect, write the letter of the correct answer to the right of the dotted line.

	Categories of Comprehension Skills								
	1 Main Idea			**2**	**3**	**4**	**5**	**6**	
	Statement a	Statement b	Statement c	Subject Matter	Supporting Details	Conclusion	Clarifying Devices	Vocabulary in Context	
Passage 1									
Passage 2									
Passage 3									
Passage 4									
Passage 5									
Passage 6									
Passage 7									
Passage 8									
Passage 9									
Passage 10									
Passage 11									
Passage 12									
Passage 13									
Passage 14									
Passage 15									
Passage 16									
Passage 17									
Passage 18									
Passage 19									
Passage 20									
Passage 21									
Passage 22									
Passage 23									
Passage 24									
Passage 25									

Diagnostic Chart: Passages 26–50

Directions: For each passage, write your answers to the left of the dotted line in the blocks for each skill category. Then correct your answers using the Answer Key on page 205. If your answer is correct, do not make any more marks in the block. If your answer is incorrect, write the letter of the correct answer to the right of the dotted line.

	Categories of Comprehension Skills								
	1 Main Idea			Subject Matter	2 Supporting Details	3 Conclusion	4 Clarifying Devices	5 Vocabulary in Context	6
	Statement a	Statement b	Statement c						
Passage 26									
Passage 27									
Passage 28									
Passage 29									
Passage 30									
Passage 31									
Passage 32									
Passage 33									
Passage 34									
Passage 35									
Passage 36									
Passage 37									
Passage 38									
Passage 39									
Passage 40									
Passage 41									
Passage 42									
Passage 43									
Passage 44									
Passage 45									
Passage 46									
Passage 47									
Passage 48									
Passage 49									
Passage 50									

Diagnostic Chart: Passages 51–75

Directions: For each passage, write your answers to the left of the dotted line in the blocks for each skill category. Then correct your answers using the Answer Key on page 206. If your answer is correct, do not make any more marks in the block. If your answer is incorrect, write the letter of the correct answer to the right of the dotted line.

	Categories of Comprehension Skills								
	1 Main Idea				2	3	4	5	6
	Statement a	Statement b	Statement c	Subject Matter	Supporting Details	Conclusion	Clarifying Devices	Vocabulary in Context	
Passage 51									
Passage 52									
Passage 53									
Passage 54									
Passage 55									
Passage 56									
Passage 57									
Passage 58									
Passage 59									
Passage 60									
Passage 61									
Passage 62									
Passage 63									
Passage 64									
Passage 65									
Passage 66									
Passage 67									
Passage 68									
Passage 69									
Passage 70									
Passage 71									
Passage 72									
Passage 73									
Passage 74									
Passage 75									

Diagnostic Chart: Passages 76–100

Directions: For each passage, write your answers to the left of the dotted line in the blocks for each skill category. Then correct your answers using the Answer Key on page 207. If your answer is correct, do not make any more marks in the block. If your answer is incorrect, write the letter of the correct answer to the right of the dotted line.

	Categories of Comprehension Skills								
	1 Main Idea				2	3	4	5	6
	Statement a	Statement b	Statement c	Subject Matter	Supporting Details	Conclusion	Clarifying Devices	Vocabulary in Context	
Passage 76									
Passage 77									
Passage 78									
Passage 79									
Passage 80									
Passage 81									
Passage 82									
Passage 83									
Passage 84									
Passage 85									
Passage 86									
Passage 87									
Passage 88									
Passage 89									
Passage 90									
Passage 91									
Passage 92									
Passage 93									
Passage 94									
Passage 95									
Passage 96									
Passage 97									
Passage 98									
Passage 99									
Passage 100									

Progress Graphs

Progress Graph: Passages 1–25

Directions: Write your Total Score for each passage in the comprehension score box under the number of the passage. Then plot your score on the graph itself by putting a small *x* on the line directly above the number of the passage, across from the score you got for that passage. As you mark your score for each passage, graph your progress by drawing a line to connect the *x*'s.

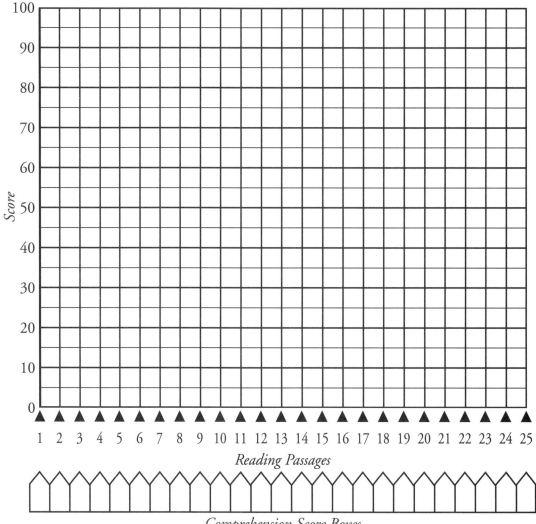

Comprehension Score Boxes

Progress Graph: Passages 26–50

Directions: Write your Total Score for each passage in the comprehension score box under the number of the passage. Then plot your score on the graph itself by putting a small *x* on the line directly above the number of the passage, across from the score you got for that passage. As you mark your score for each passage, graph your progress by drawing a line to connect the *x*'s.

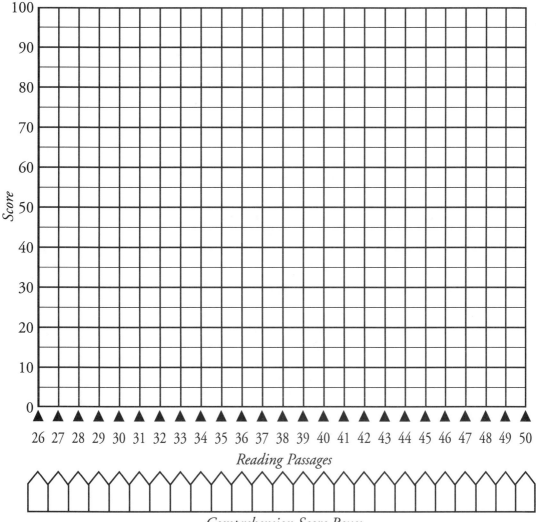

Reading Passages

Comprehension Score Boxes

Progress Graph: Passages 51–75

Directions: Write your Total Score for each passage in the comprehension score box under the number of the passage. Then plot your score on the graph itself by putting a small *x* on the line directly above the number of the passage, across from the score you got for that passage. As you mark your score for each passage, graph your progress by drawing a line to connect the *x*'s.

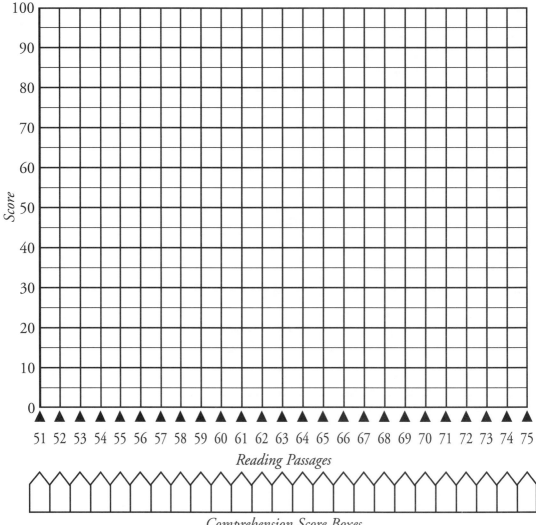

Reading Passages

Comprehension Score Boxes

Progress Graph: Passages 76–100

Directions: Write your Total Score for each passage in the comprehension score box under the number of the passage. Then plot your score on the graph itself by putting a small *x* on the line directly above the number of the passage, across from the score you got for that passage. As you mark your score for each passage, graph your progress by drawing a line to connect the *x*'s.

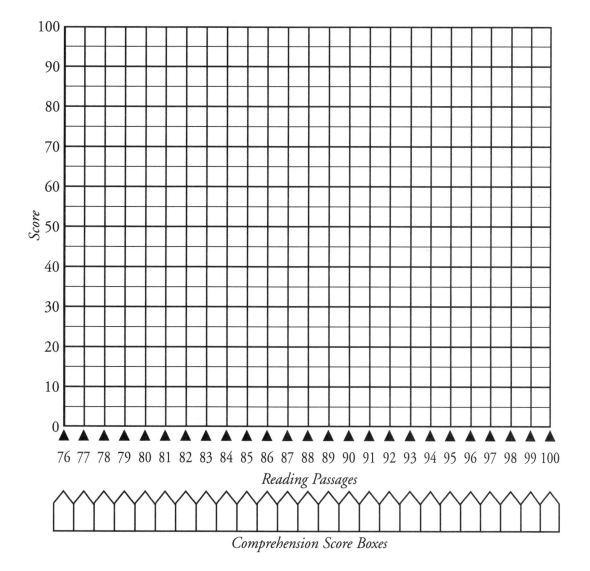

Reading Passages

Comprehension Score Boxes